*The Private Life of
Sherlock Holmes*

VINCENT STARRETT

THE PRIVATE LIFE OF

SHERLOCK

HOLMES

OTTO
PENZLER
BOOKS

NEW YORK

Copyright © 1930, 1932, 1933 by Vincent Starrett

First published in 1933 by The Macmillan Company

Otto Penzler Books, 129 W. 56th Street,
New York, NY 10019 (Editorial Offices Only)

Macmillan Publishing Company, 866 Third Avenue,
New York, NY 10022

Maxwell Macmillan Canada, Inc., 1200 Eglinton Avenue East,
Suite 200, Don Mills, Ontario M3C 3N1

Macmillan Publishing Company is part of the Maxwell
Communication Group of Companies.

Library of Congress Cataloging-in-Publication Data
Starrett, Vincent, 1886–1974.
    The private life of Sherlock Holmes / Vincent Starrett.
        p.   cm.
    ISBN 1-883402-05-0
    1. Doyle, Arthur Conan, Sir, 1859–1930—Characters—Sherlock
Holmes. 2. Detective and mystery stories, English—History and
criticism. 3. Holmes, Sherlock (Fictitious character) 4. Private
investigators in literature. I. Title.
    PR4624.S8   1993   93-19718   CIP
    823'.8-dc20

10   9   8   7   6   5   4   3   2   1

Printed in the United States of America

Acknowledgment

IT WOULD be difficult, not to say impossible, to acknowledge every published line which may have influenced the author's thought in connection with the making of this book; but one's gratitude is chiefly due a certain John H. Watson, M.D., erstwhile of London, England. More specifically one is grateful to his surrogate, the late Sir Arthur Conan Doyle; and to Lady Conan Doyle and the estate of Sir Arthur, by whose gracious permission this volume is made possible. Formal—and grateful —acknowledgment is also made as follows: to Messrs. Harper & Brothers, publishers of *The Adventures of Sherlock Holmes*, copyright 1892, and *The Memoirs of Sherlock Holmes*, copyright 1894; to Messrs. Doubleday, Doran and Company, publishers of *The Hound of the Baskervilles*, copyright 1902; *The Return of Sherlock Holmes*, copyright 1905; *The Valley of Fear*, copyright 1914; *His Last Bow*, copyright 1917, and *The Case Book of Sherlock Holmes*, copyright 1927; to Messrs. Little, Brown & Company, of Boston, the publishers of *Memories and Adventures*, Sir Arthur's autobiography; to *Life and Letters* (London) and London *Punch,* in the pages of which admirable journals originally appeared the delightful Examination Papers reproduced in this volume; to Messrs. Desmond MacCarthy and E. V. Knox in person; and, again, to Messrs. Doubleday, Doran and Company, of New York, publishers of *The Case of Oscar Slater.* Several of the present chapters first appeared in American journals, to the editors of which acknowledgment is made as follows: to the *Atlantic Monthly,* for *Enter Mr. Sherlock Holmes;* to *Real Detective Tales,* for *No. 221-B Baker Street;* to the *Golden Book,* for *The Real Sherlock Holmes;* and to the *Bookman* for *The Private Life of Sherlock Holmes* and *Ave Sherlock Morituri et Cetera.* Individually, one must mention, here as elsewhere, three eminent Sherlockians without whose help in special matters this volume would have been a poorer tribute to its subject; they are Mr. William Gillette, the great American actor, Mr. Frederic Dorr Steele, the great American illustrator, and Dr. Gray Chandler Briggs, the well-known roentgenologist of St. Louis. For the rest, the bibliography which closes the volume will suggest somewhat of the debt one owes to Messrs. Maurice, Roberts, Rogers, Bangs, *et al;* no doubt to others who are not specifically mentioned. Yet one would also—for all of this—suggest that these chapters are in no small degree part of the heart and mind of him who types this foreword.

V. S.

Contents

Illustrations

TO

WILLIAM GILLETTE

FREDERIC DORR STEELE

AND

GRAY CHANDLER BRIGGS

IN GRATITUDE

Enter Mr. Sherlock Holmes

THE London "season" of the year 1886, upon its surface, was much as other and similar seasons had been before it. No blare of sudden trumpets marked its advent. Victoria was still placidly upon her throne; Lord Salisbury—for the second time—had ousted Gladstone from the premier's chair; Ireland was seething with outrage and sedition, and Beecham's Pills were "universally admitted to be a marvellous antidote for nervous disorders." In literature the gods, perhaps, were Stevenson and Henry James and Henty, depending upon one's age; but an Irishman named Wilde was making himself a figure of fantastic moment by his championship of aestheticism. At the Gaiety, Mr. Cellier's *Dorothy* had begun its celebrated run of 968 performances, and *The Harbor Lights* were gleaming brightly at the Adelphi. In Piccadilly the race of hansom cabs was swift and dangerous. No wars immediately threatened; the wide world was at peace. A smug and happy time, a time of prosperity and great contentment. And no celestial phenomena existed to indicate that, once more in the history of the world, a blue moon was marking an epochal event.

Certainly no planets fell to tell an impoverished provincial doctor, resident at Southsea, Portsmouth, that he had brought forth a new immortal in the world of letters.

Sherlock Holmes, however, was already in the world. With a Dr. Watson, late of the 5th Northumberland Fusiliers, he had engaged a suite of rooms at No. 221-B Baker Street, London, and entered upon his astonishing career as a consulting detective. As far as the world is concerned, he is there yet.

*   *   *

Times had not been of the best for Dr. A. Conan Doyle of Bush Villa, Southsea. The young man had recently married, and was eking out the slender returns of early medical practice by writing stories for the magazines. It had occurred to him that he might go on writing short stories forever and make no headway. What was necessary, he was certain, if one intended to be an author, was to get one's name upon the cover of a book. A first novel —*The Firm of Girdlestone*—had been an impressive failure, and was still in manuscript about the house. But he had, for some time, been turning in his mind the possibility of something new and fresh in the literature of detection. Gaboriau had pleased him by the precision of his plots, and a boyhood hero had been the Chevalier C. Auguste Dupin, Poe's masterful amateur detective. What was there, he asked himself, that he—Doyle—could bring to this field, which would be indubitably his own?

Outside, over his door, at night, burned the red lamp that was the sign of his profession. In the daylight, his brass name plate—polished every morning—shone brightly in the Portsmouth sun. But the patients that either of them should have attracted were few and far between. In his patients' sitting room—three chairs, a table, and a patch of carpet—as he smoked and thought, there rose before him the remembered image of his former teacher at the university—one Joseph Bell, "thin, wiry, dark, with a high-nosed acute face, penetrating grey eyes, angular shoulders," and a peculiar walk. Joseph Bell, M.D., F.R.C.S., Edinburgh; consulting surgeon to the Royal Infirmary and Royal Hospital for Sick Children, whose voice was high and discordant, whose skill as a surgeon was profound, and whose uncanny trick of diagnosis was a legend of the institution. It occurred to the young physician, waiting for his patients who did not come, that if Joseph Bell had determined to be a detective, he would have reduced "this fascinating but unorganized business to something nearer an exact science."

Bell, for reasons which Doyle the student had never quite understood, had singled him out from among the droves of others who frequented the wards, and made him his out-patient clerk. It was not an onerous position. The student herded the waiting patients into line, made simple notes of their cases, and ushered them into the big room in which Bell sat in state. But it had been quickly evident to young Arthur Conan Doyle that Joseph Bell learned more about the patients at a glance than he, the questioner, had learned with all his questions.

"He would sit in his receiving room," wrote Doyle the novelist, later in life, "with a face like a red Indian, and diagnose the people as they came in, before they even opened their mouths. He would tell them their symptoms, and even give them details of their past life; and hardly ever would he make a mistake."

The results were often highly dramatic. To a civilian patient, on one occasion, he observed: "Well, my man, you've served in the army."

"Aye, sir."

"Not long discharged?"

"No, sir."

"A Highland regiment?"

"Aye, sir."

"A non-com. officer?"

"Aye, sir."

"Stationed at Barbados?"

"Aye, sir."

"You see, gentlemen," explained the physician to his surrounding students and dressers, "the man was a respectful man but did not remove his hat. They do not in the army; but he would have

DR. JOSEPH BELL OF EDINBURGH
From whom Sir Arthur Conan Doyle drew his first portrait
of Sherlock Holmes.

learned civilian ways if he had been long discharged. He has an air of authority, and he is obviously Scottish. As to Barbados, his complaint is elephantiasis, which is West Indian and not British."[1]

And no little of the dry humour of Joseph Bell's deductions is visible in another case that is of record.

"What is the matter with this man, sir?" he suddenly inquired of a trembling student, standing by. "Come down, sir, and look at him. No, you mustn't touch him. Use your eyes, sir! Use your ears, use your brain, use your bump of perception, use your powers of deduction!"

The stammering student did his best: "Hip-joint disease, sir?"

"Hip-nothing!" retorted Bell disgustedly. "The man's limp is not from his hip but from his foot, or rather from his feet. Were you to observe closely you would note that there are slits—cut by a knife —in those parts of the shoes on which the pressure of the shoe is greatest against the foot. The man is suffering from corns, gentlemen, and has no hip trouble at all. But he has not come to us to be treated for corns, gentlemen; we are not chiropodists. His trouble is of a more serious nature. This is a case of chronic alcoholism, gentlemen. The rubicund nose, the puffed and bloated face, the bloodshot eyes, the tremulous hands and twitching

[1] A. C. Doyle: *Memories and Adventures.*

face muscles, with the quick, pulsating temporal arteries, all combine to show us this. But these deductions, gentlemen, must be confirmed by absolute and concrete evidence. In this instance, my diagnosis is confirmed by the neck of a whisky bottle protruding from the patient's right-hand pocket." [1]

Of another patient, he once said: "Gentlemen, we have here a man who is either a cork-cutter or a slater. If you will use your eyes a moment, you will be able to define a slight hardening—a regular callus, gentlemen—on one side of his forefinger, and a thickening on the outer side of the thumb; a sure sign that he follows the one occupation or the other." [2]

And of still another, he observed: "Gentlemen, a fisherman! You will note that, although it is a summer's day, and very hot, the patient is wearing top boots. When he sat upon the chair they were plainly visible. No one but a sailor would wear top boots at this season of the year. The shade of tan upon his face shows him to be a coastwise, not a deep-sea sailor who makes foreign lands. His tan is that produced by one climate only—it is a local tan. A knife scabbard shows beneath his coat, the kind used by fishermen in this part of the world. He is concealing a quid of tobacco in the farthest corner of his mouth, and he manages it very adroitly in-

---

[1] H. E. Jones: *The Original of Sherlock Holmes.*
[2] *Ibid.*

deed, gentlemen. The sum of these deductions is that he is a fisherman. Further to prove the correctness of my diagnosis, I notice a number of fish-scales adhering to his clothes and hands, while the odour of fish announced his arrival in a most marked and striking manner." [1]

To the wondering Watsons it was all very marvellous indeed.

* * *

Waiting and smoking in his sitting room at Southsea for the patients that seldom came, young Dr. Conan Doyle heard again the strident voice of his former mentor, haranguing the awkward students of Edinburgh's school of medicine. In one familiar and oft-repeated apophthegm there was the very substance of a new detective. . . .

"From close observation and deduction, gentlemen, it is possible to make a diagnosis that will be correct in any and every case. However, you must not neglect to ratify your deductions, to substantiate your diagnoses, with the stethoscope and by all other recognized and every-day methods." [2]

Out of his memories of Joseph Bell, hawk-faced and a trifle eerie for all his sardonic humour, the creator of Sherlock Holmes builded the outlines of his great detective. But it was an outline only; it was the special genius of Conan Doyle, himself, that was to enable him to complete the picture. It

---

[1] H. E. Jones: *The Original of Sherlock Holmes.*
[2] Joseph Bell: *"Mr. Sherlock Holmes."*

was from the first, indeed, only the potentialities of a living Sherlock Holmes latent within his medical creator that made possible the gaunt detective's entrance upon the foggy stage of London's wickedness.

The name, one fancies, was an inspiration. To think of Sherlock Holmes by any other name is, paradoxically, unthinkable. It was a matter, apparently, that gave the author only slight concern. Obviously, his detective must not be "Mr. Sharps" or "Mr. Ferrets"; good taste rebelled against so elementary a nomenclature. His love for the American essayist—also a physician—dictated the choice at one end: "Never," he later wrote, "have I so known and loved a man whom I had never seen."[1] But Sherlock was longer in coming. A leaf from a notebook of the period exists, and the astonished eye beholds it with dismay. "Sherrinford Holmes" was the detective's name as first it was jotted down by the man who was to create him. And from the same source, one is permitted to deduce an earlier thought than "Watson." The good Watson, one learns with tardy apprehension, was to have been "Ormond Sacker." It is a revealing page, that page from Conan Doyle's old notebook, and a faintly distressing one. In the end, however, it was Sherlock Holmes,[2] and Sherlock Holmes it is to-day—

[1] A. C. Doyle: *Through the Magic Door.*

[2] "Years ago," Conan Doyle was once quoted in a newspaper, "I made thirty runs against a bowler by the name of Sherlock, and I always had a kindly feeling for that name."

the most familiar figure in modern English fiction; a name that has become a permanent part of the English language.

*　　*　　*

It was late in the year 1880, or perhaps early in 1881, that Holmes and Watson met and discovered their common need of the moment, which was a comfortable suite of rooms at a figure that would suit their pocketbooks. One inclines to the latter date, in view of the recorded fact that it was as late as March the fourth in 1881, that Holmes revealed his profession to his fellow-lodger. Devotees will recall the passage in *A Study in Scarlet* in which the revelation is set forth; but one fancies that early readers of that first adventure must have come upon it much as Crusoe came upon the footprint in the sand.

Young Stamford introduced them, then vanished from the tale, his whole existence justified. The day following, they inspected the rooms in Baker Street and took them on the spot.

It is amazing that the good doctor did not guess the truth about his new acquaintance weeks before he was told. Yet by that very failure to suspect he was forever to establish himself in the character of Watson. That first meeting, indeed, was to establish a tradition of the saga—a bit of dialogue which was, in essence, to be a sort of prologue to every tale that was to follow. The doctor's record of the lines is quite precise:—

"Dr. Watson, Mr. Sherlock Holmes," said Stamford, introducing us.

"How are you?" he said cordially, gripping my hand with a strength for which I should hardly have given him credit. "You have been in Afghanistan, I perceive."

"How on earth did you know that?" I asked in astonishment.

"The Lauriston Gardens Mystery," it will be recalled, followed quickly on the heels of Holmes's confession that he was a consulting detective—perhaps the only one in the world; and for the first time, under the eyes of his admiring Boswell, the greatest detective of history or fiction set forth upon his mission of humane vengeance. It was a perfect morning for the adventure—that is, "it was a foggy, cloudy morning, and a dun-coloured veil hung over the house-tops, looking like the reflection of the mud-coloured streets beneath." And a man named Enoch Drebber, of Cleveland, U.S.A., or so his cards revealed, was dead in dreadful circumstances, in a house at No. 3, comma, Lauriston Gardens, a trifle off the Brixton Road.

Thus opened the strange case of Jefferson Hope, for which Gregson and Lestrade, of Scotland Yard, received the credit, but which was solved by Mr. Sherlock Holmes of Baker Street, and later set forth

Study in Scarlet

Ormond Sacker - ~~from Soudan~~ from Afghanistan
        Lived at 221 B Upper Baker Street
with
    J Sherrinford Holmes -
            The Laws of Evidence

    Reserved -
Sleepy eyed young man - philosopher - Collector of rare Violins
An Amati -   Chemical Laboratory
        I have four hundred a year -

I am a Consulting detective -

What rot this is " I cried - throwing the volume

    petulantly aside " I must say that I have no
patience with people who build up fine theories in their
own armchairs which can never be reduced to
practice -
                Lecoq was a bungler -
    Dupin was better. Dupin was decidedly smart -
His trick of following a train of thought was more
sensational than clever but still he had analytical

THE GENESIS OF SHERLOCK HOLMES.

by his friend and companion, Dr. John H. Watson, who had all the facts in his journal. It is an admirable bit of melodrama, well told in vigorous, Anglo-Saxon English, delayed in the middle by a secondary story that is reminiscent of Bret Harte at his worst, and ending on the inevitable explanation of the detective.

The book was written in the Spring of 1886 and by July had been returned by Arrowsmith, unread. "Two or three others sniffed and turned away." The friendly editor of the *Cornhill Magazine*, who had paid £30 for a much shorter tale, some time before, found it at once too short and too long. On the point of laying it away beside its predecessor, *The Firm of Girdlestone*, the despairing author bethought himself of yet another publisher who might be cozened. Thus near was Sherlock Holmes to dying at his birth.

Ward, Lock & Company received the tattered manuscript and looked it over, and on the last day of October Dr. Conan Doyle, gloomily smoking in his patients' sitting room, received a letter:

"Dear Sir—We have read your story and are pleased with it. We could not publish it this year as the market is flooded at present with cheap fiction, but if you do not object to its being held over till next year, we will give you £25 for the copyright."

It was not a tempting offer, even for so impecunious a practitioner as Dr. Conan Doyle. Sick at heart, however, by repeated disappointments, he wrote a letter of acceptance, and the deed was done. Sherlock Holmes was committed to the publishers, the pirates, and the world; and *A Study in Scarlet* became the issue of *Beeton's Christmas Annual* for 1887. At no time, the author tells us in his autobiography, did he receive another penny for it. Yet so many times has it been reprinted and pirated and otherwise put forth, in many lands, that a very decent income might have been achieved from that first slender volume—when later volumes had been written—if only its author might have kept his title.

That lurid paper-back of Christmas 1887 is to-day one of the rarest books of modern times—a keystone sought by discriminating collectors in every part of the earth. Of equal rarity, and possibly even more difficult to find, is the second edition of the tale, with illustrations by the author's father. It was issued in 1888, with a brief publisher's preface that is a masterpiece of inept rhetoric and comparison. "The *Study in Scarlet* and the unravelling of the apparently unfathomable mystery by the cool shrewdness of Mr. Sherlock Holmes," the reader was informed, "yield nothing in point of sustained interest and gratified expectation to the best stories of the school that has produced 'Mr. Barnes of New York,' 'Shadowed by Three,' &c., &c."

The line drawings by Charles Doyle are astounding, viewed at this date. One wonders what his son thought of them, even in 1888. But Dr. Conan Doyle's kindness of heart is perhaps attested by their inclusion.

* * *

British literature in the eighties had a considerable vogue in America, and much of it for a simple reason. No copyright act existed, and it was possible to publish it for nothing. But publication, even under these unfavorable auspices, had helped to make a number of reputations. Among the reputations thus established, in some degree, was that of Dr. Conan Doyle. In England, *A Study in Scarlet* had received some favorable but unvociferous comment; in America it was no inconsiderable success. Thus it happened that, in 1889, when *Micah Clarke* had been praised by Andrew Lang and published to the world, to mark its author's versatility, there appeared in London an agent for the American house of Lippincott, with knowledge of that author's previous work.

At a dinner paid for by the American, there were present by invitation Oscar Wilde himself, a garrulous member of Parliament named Gill, and the still impecunious physician from Portsmouth. Wilde's conversation was a delight,[1] and as a result of the eventful evening the happy authors were

[1] So much so that Mr. H. W. Bell believes it influenced some of the early pages of *The Sign of Four*—notably in the description of Thaddeus Sholto's house and conversation, and in similar detail.

ENTER MR. SHERLOCK HOLMES
Front wrapper of the rare first edition of *A Study in Scarlet*

commissioned to write books for *Lippincott's Magazine.* Wilde's contribution was *The Picture of Dorian Gray,* and Doyle's was *The Sign of Four,* in which Sherlock Holmes, for the second time—under the eyes of Watson—went forth into the London fogs upon a trail of violence and murder.

The adventure is dated September 1888; and the tale appeared in the issue of *Lippincott's Magazine* for February 1890. Are there any who, having read it, can now forget it? It is still perhaps the most vivid and the best of all the many tales that were to follow, and far, far better than the one that had preceded it. Of course, "the day had been a dreary one, and a dense drizzly fog lay low upon the great city. Mud-coloured clouds drooped sadly over the muddy streets. Down the Strand the lamps were but misty splotches of diffused light which threw a feeble circular glimmer upon the slimy pavement."

And through this melancholy glamour, in a four-wheeler, drove Watson and Sherlock Holmes, with Mary Morstan by their side, to a rendezvous beside the third pillar of the Lyceum, and thence to Pondicherry Lodge and the horror of the grinning Face.

It was Jones, this time, who took the credit—Athelney Jones, you will recall, of Scotland Yard—and for Watson, at the end of the trail, there was a wife. For Holmes there remained the bottle of cocaine that stood upon his shelf, toward which, when all was over, his long white hand was slowly reaching up.

The book appeared in the autumn of 1890, over the imprint of Spencer Blackett, and was popular from the first. It, too, to-day is rare and difficult to find. But the money that it made for its author was insufficient for his needs, and Dr. Conan Doyle continued to practice medicine at Southsea. A second great historical novel, meanwhile, had been written—the doctor's industry was incredible—and *The White Company* was all but ready to take its place beside the earlier *Micah Clarke*. That Sherlock Holmes would again appear between the covers of a book did not enter the author's mind, save perhaps as a happy possibility—when and if some other publisher, greatly daring, should solicit Watson for another reminiscence.

Dr. Conan Doyle, for all his mounting reputation, was a modest man, and still a man of medicine who wrote novels when his profession did not pay. In the latter days of 1890, indeed, he was contemplating a happy union of his two vocations.

As a specialist, it occurred to him, he would have leisure for his writing and perhaps command a greater flow of patients; wherefore, he would to Vienna go and study to be a specialist! The die was cast, and as the year drew to its close, Dr. and Mrs. Arthur Conan Doyle closed the doors of Bush Villa behind them, for the last time. There is, to-day, one reads, a tablet on the villa, and "Doyle

House" is a place of tourist interest. As the birth-place, so to speak, of Sherlock Holmes, it should be marked, one thinks, by national decree.

*   *   *

With the Spring, his work in Vienna completed, a new eye specialist tacked his plate over a door in Devonshire Place, not far from classical Harley Street, and the new chapter of adversity was begun. "Every morning," wrote Dr. Conan Doyle, later on in life, "I walked from my lodgings in Montague Place, reached my consulting-room at ten, and sat there until three or four, with never a ring to disturb my serenity."

It was a situation made to order for literary work. A number of popular monthlies had begun to make their appearance on the stands, among them the famous *Strand*. To the thoughtfully smoking doctor, it appeared that a serial might be an impediment in such a journal, but that a series of short tales, featuring a single individual who would appear throughout the series, might be the very ticket. And, happily, the individual was at hand. In the long hours of waiting, all unknowing whither it was to lead him, Dr. Conan Doyle, eye specialist, of No. 2, Devonshire Place, began to write his remarkable series of short detective tales, now famous the world over as *The Adventures of Sherlock Holmes*.

This time Holmes was in the world to stay. That

lean and sinewy figure was to become a symbol as familiar as the Nelson Monument and the Tower of London. A figure of incredible popularity, who exists in history more surely than the warriors and statesmen in whose time he lived and had his being. An illusion so real, as Father Ronald Knox has happily suggested,[1] that one might some day look about for him in Heaven, forgetting that he was only a character in a book.

[1] Ronald A. Knox: *Essays in Satire.*

The Methods of
Mr. Sherlock Holmes

To THE earnest student of the Holmes saga it must be clear that the medical practice of Dr. Watson, after his marriage, was never at any time excessive. For a while it was substantial and satisfactory; but at no time, apparently, was it so heavy that, at a call from Sherlock Holmes, it could not be dropped for a day or two, or turned over to an accommodating neighbor. Watson, himself, we may be sure, for all his felicity, thought often and with great happiness of his days at Baker Street, when he was a figure in events of tempestuous moment; and if he wavered in the face of duty, there was always his wife to urge him to listen to the siren call of adventure. Anstruther, or another, she was always certain, would do his work for him. "You are so interested in Mr. Sherlock Holmes's cases," she used to say.

Precious little urging, one fancies, the good doctor ever needed. He could pack in half an hour, and there was always a convenient train from Paddington or some place.

Watson, at the close of the grim adventure called

The Sign of Four, it will be remembered, had won the heart and hand of Mary Morstan, and the marriage must have followed almost immediately. There is, unfortunately, a confusion of dates at this point, which whimsical scholars have striven to correct, not with entire success. It is certain that at the time of the first of the recorded *Adventures of Sherlock Holmes*—the curious reminiscence known as *A Scandal in Bohemia*—Holmes and the doctor had not seen each other for some months. Yet the adventure is quite precisely dated in March of the year 1888: it was on the night of the 20th that Watson, returning from a professional visit, passed the rooms in Baker Street, saw the spare figure of his friend "pass twice in dark silhouette against the blind," and was filled with an irresistible desire to look in upon him.

If Watson's memory of this evening is correct, it is obvious that it was at fault when indirectly he gave date to the earlier adventure of *The Sign of Four,* which immediately preceded his marriage yet was dated in the month of September, 1888. And still other adventures, recorded later in the series, by their dating only increase the confusion. A plausible explanation of the difficulty must be found either in the suggestion that Watson himself was a bit confused about the date of his engagement and marriage, or in the perhaps more likely supposition that Dr. Conan Doyle was careless in the matter.

Possibly it is unimportant. The pleasing fact is that a certain Mr. Greenhough Smith was editor of the *Strand Magazine*, at just the proper moment, and welcomed the further reminiscences of Dr. Watson with flattering enthusiasm. It was in the seventh number of that journal, dated July, 1891, that the first of the series appeared, and by the time the last was published, in the Christmas issue of 1893, the name and fame of Sherlock Holmes was known around the world.

* * *

But on that night of March, in 1888, for Holmes and Watson the curtain was just ringing up. The gaunt detective was glad to see his friend again, after their separation, although "his manner was not effusive." That he was at work upon a problem had been evident to Watson even from the street. The shadow on the blind had told its tale: "He was pacing the room swiftly, eagerly, with his head sunk upon his chest, and his hands clasped behind him. He was at work again. He had risen from his drug-created dreams, and was hot upon the scent of some new problem."

What that problem was, the world recalls. The surprising individual whose letter had preceded him, and who was to arrive at a quarter before eight, was punctual. His knock upon the door was loud and authoritative. His stature was not less than six feet, six inches. His dress was astounding in its barbaric opulence, and he must have been an astonishing figure, indeed, even in *fin de siècle* London. "Heavy bands of Astrakhan were slashed across the sleeves and fronts of his double-breasted coat, while the deep blue cloak which was thrown over his shoulders was lined with flame-coloured silk, and secured at the neck with a brooch which consisted of a single flaming beryl." His boots, which extended halfway up his calves, were trimmed at the tops with rich brown fur; and to complete the Stevensonian melodrama of his appearance, he wore a black vizard mask across the upper part of his face, "extending down past the cheek-bones."

He had not spoken, however, before Holmes was aware that he was addressing Wilhelm Gottsreich Sigismond von Ormstein, Grand Duke of Cassel-Felstein and hereditary King of Bohemia.

In the singular adventure that followed the appearance of this royal apparition—"the comedy of the King's photograph," it has been called—Holmes rose to heights of admirable ingenuity, even though in the end he failed. Defeated by a woman! It is the only defeat of its kind in the long history of the great detective's career; and to Holmes, thereafter, Irene Norton (née Adler), of dubious memory, was always *the* woman. But the King was satisfied; and Watson was to record, in future, only a brilliant sequence of successes.

It is just conceivable that implicit in this first

"short adventure," that is to say, in this first of Watson's reminiscences in the shorter form, we have all that is essentially important in the saga of Sherlock Holmes. Be that as it may—and one does not insist upon the notion—it is an excellent tale, with all the glamour of the others, plus an admirable sense of the rooms in Baker Street and a delightful glimpse of the two friends working in collaboration. In so far as Watson himself, as narrator, is concerned, it contains much of what was later to become a favorite formula in the telling of these adventures. It is practically all on exhibition—the Baker Street prologue with mystifications by the detective; the references to other cases whose secrets may not at the moment be revealed; the statement of the problem about to present itself, and discussion of the insufficient evidence at hand; the arrival of the illustrious client, with further mystifications and an elaboration of the problem; the adventure itself, and finally the fascinating if slightly anti-climactic explanations of the detective, illustrating the ease with which it all had been accomplished.

Others among the reminiscences are perhaps more rigid examples of the formula, which—after all—was just beginning to shape itself in *A Scandal in Bohemia,* but few are better stories. For good measure, there are vivid, first-hand glimpses of Holmes's "amazing powers in the use of disguises," which in later tales are more often referred to than they are shown in operation. It may well be, indeed, that the narrative lacks only a corpse or two of being quite the best of all the adventures. But the great fathomer's debt to Poe is very evident throughout. For all his earlier and perhaps ill-considered gibing at Dupin (in *A Study in Scarlet*), it is to be noted that in *A Scandal in Bohemia* Holmes was not above taking a leaf from the book of that "very inferior fellow." The incident of Watson's smoke-rocket, and the false alarm of fire at Briony Lodge, could only have been a happy memory of the duplicity of M. Dupin in the case of the celebrated *Purloined Letter*. There was always just a touch of professional jealousy in Holmes's character—entirely natural, no doubt— that even Watson could not gloss away.

* * *

In the twenty-three further reminiscences contributed thereafter by Watson, through Conan Doyle, to the *Strand*, it is evident that a sort of intermittent partnership with Holmes had been resumed. The order of the adventures is not, however, chronological, and further doubts are possible as to Watson's memory. The dating is almost irritatingly insufficient. While in the main the biographical narrative marches continuously, there are many backward glances, and it is obvious that a number of the problems are recollections of the days that preceded the doctor's marriage, when he and Holmes were still fellow-lodgers in Baker Street. A chronological table of the adventures, accurately dated, is not possible, although the talents of a number of scholars have been directed toward the compilation of such a table—notably those of Mr. H. W. Bell, Mr. Thomas S. Blakeney, and Mr. S. C. Roberts, who are not always in agreement.

But what a record of achievement they reveal! What a picture they disclose of London at the century's end! Is it too much to claim that social historians in the years to come are more likely to return to Watson than to the dull McCarthy and the sardonic Strachey? Of all the annalists of that curious time one must prefer the humble Watson, with his chronicle of crime and detection and his swift, kaleidoscopic record of bowler hats and "kerridges," of bicycles and Turkish Baths, of green November fogs and baking August sunshines. No telephones had been installed to complicate the business of life; when Holmes made haste he sent a telegram. In every doorway lurked the minions of the Yard. The picture is unforgettable and unique. "Baker Street," says Mr. Roberts, "remains for ever permeated with the Watsonian aura. The dim figures of the Baker Street irregulars scuttle through the November gloom; the ghostly hansom drives away, bearing Holmes and Watson on an errand of mystery." [1]

Queer folk came to the rooms of Sherlock

[1] S. C. Roberts: *Doctor Watson.*

Holmes in Baker Street, and always they came when they were in trouble. It was a grim business that occupied the talents of the great detective. There was the dreadful case of Helen Stoner, recalled by Watson from an earlier year—the shocking adventure of *The Speckled Band;* and that gruesome business of *The Engineer's Thumb,* which marked the summer of 1889. And the hideous adventure of *The Copper Beeches* that all but cost Miss Violet Hunter her life. One recalls the surprising episode of the managing director of the Franco-Midland Hardware Company, who knocked on his own door with his heels; and the alarming experience of *The Greek Interpreter*—a curious problem that was called to Holmes's attention by his brother Mycroft. The singular adventure of *The Red-Headed League,* to be sure, was pure comedy to begin with, but it ended in the capture of the criminal upon whom Inspector Athelney Jones would rather have clapped bracelets than any man in London.

* * *

Throughout all, the remarkable methods of Mr. Sherlock Holmes are admirably in evidence; they are, of course, the *raison d'être* of Watson's reminiscences. And they are, clearly enough, the principles and tenets of Dr. Joseph Bell of Edinburgh, a bit stretched and dramatized, applied to specially selected cases of—for the most part—fantastic crime.

In them, one hears again the dry inflections of the Scottish doctor, laying down his broad rules of diagnosis. . . .

"Try to learn the features of a disease or injury, gentlemen, as precisely as you know the features, the gait, the tricks of manner of your most intimate friend. Him, even in a crowd, you can recognize at once. It may be a crowd of men dressed all alike, and each having his full complement of eyes, nose, hair, and limbs. In every essential they resemble one another; only in trifles do they differ— and yet, by knowing these trifles well, you make your recognition or your diagnosis with ease. So it is with disease of mind or body or morals. Racial peculiarities, hereditary tricks of manner, accent, occupation or the want of it, education, environment of every kind, by their little trivial impressions gradually mould or carve the individual, and leave finger marks or chisel scores which the expert can detect. The great broad characteristics which at a glance can be recognized as indicative of heart disease or consumption, chronic drunkenness or long-continued loss of blood, are the common property of the veriest tyro in medicine, while to masters of their art there are myriads of signs eloquent and instructive, but which need the educated eye to discover. . . . The importance of the infinitely little is incalculable. Poison a well at Mecca with the cholera bacillus, and the holy water which the pilgrims carry off in bottles will infect a continent.

The rags of the victims of a plague will terrify every seaport in Christendom." [1]

These are the accents of Sherlock Holmes himself. It is amusing to recall, however, that Dr. Joseph Bell, pleased by the success of the detective for whom he sat as model, in later years suggested problems to Dr. Conan Doyle, which were not—the author admits in his autobiography—very practical. But Bell's appreciation of the immortal Holmes was keen, and his own description of the detective is very adroit: "A shrewd, quick-sighted, inquisitive man, half doctor, half virtuoso, with plenty of spare time, a retentive memory, and perhaps with the best gift of all—the power of unloading the mind of all the burden of trying to remember unnecessary details."

Holmes looked upon himself, it is to be recalled, as a machine. When he does not suggest it, himself, the excellent Watson—like a Greek Chorus—does it for him. Thus at the outset of the *Adventures,* and not then for the first time, we are reminded that "all emotions . . . were abhorrent to his cold, precise, but admirably balanced mind. He was, I take it, the most perfect reasoning and observing machine that the world has seen." Deduction, of course, was his principal tool of office, and seldom was he at fault. Observation was a close and important second, but it was not always necessary for Holmes to *see* to understand. Pipe in mouth,

[1] Joseph Bell: *"Mr. Sherlock Holmes."*

his eyes half closed or shut entirely, he could listen to a client's tale of puzzling horror and know the answer to the problem before the man had finished speaking. Whatever he might reveal to Watson, in advance of the ultimate revelation, reading the doctor's account of a recital in Baker Street one is always certain that Holmes, himself, is hot upon the track. A particularly difficult case was some-times a "three-pipe problem," after the client had departed; but with Holmes of all people difficulty was a very relative word indeed.

The importance of tobacco in Holmes's scheme of life and thought, incidentally, has been pointed out by all students of the detective's methods. "He is," as Father Knox cheerfully admits, "one of the world's great smokers." [1] But while occasionally he tossed a cigar case to Watson, he himself alter-nated between a pipe and cigarettes. The pipe was largely for his problems. In ordinary conversation, or when time was short, an occasional cigarette was sufficient. In practically all of the tales there is the odour of tobacco smoke. The rooms in Baker Street must always have been full of it.

The drugs—cocaine and morphine—with which, during the early days of his association with Wat-son, he used to "stimulate" and "clarify" his mind, were seldom necessary during the *Adventures,* one is glad to know—a reform for which Watson was, in large part, responsible.

[1] Ronald A. Knox: *Essays in Satire.*

The familiar Baker Street pose of lounging indifference, in tweeds or dressing gown, however, only masked the turnings of his restless mind. Bursts of almost daemonic enterprise followed quickly, as a rule. In pursuit, he had amazing energy. Holmes at his utmost must indeed have been a sight to strike the Scotland Yarders stiff with wonder and dismay. Sometimes on hands and knees he traced a culprit's spoor across a sodden garden; and indoors, it is recorded, he often lay flat upon the boards, with glass or measuring line in hand, to verify his suspicions in the flagrant minutiae of a room's disorder. An astonishing spectacle. But there is nothing self-conscious about a machine dedicated to vengeance and retribution. Enviable was the humble rôle of John H. Watson, whose privilege it was to watch; while Gregson and the others sneered. . . .

Granted the opportunity, gentlemen—one might cry, in paraphrase of Dr. Bell—of recovering a single day out of the irrecoverable past, how would you choose to spend that sorcerous gift? With Master Shakespeare in his tiring room? With Villon and his companions of the cockleshell? Riding with Rupert or barging it with Cleopatra up the Nile? Or would you choose to squander it on a chase with Sherlock Holmes, after a visit to the rooms in Baker Street? There can be only one possible answer, gentlemen, to the question.

* * *

DR. A. CONAN DOYLE OF BUSH VILLA, SOUTHSEA

The notable taste of Mr. Sherlock Holmes for theatrical arrangement and dramatic effects has been a subject of frequent comment; and so, too, has been his flair for sardonic epigram. His theatricality is evident in all of the adventures. It is his most human failing—his appreciation of applause. It is the actor ranting to his audience when he cries: "Gentlemen, let me introduce you to the famous black pearl of the Borgias!" It is the admirable manipulator of third-act surprises who serves up the missing naval papers, under cover, as a breakfast dish. In the matter of epigram, he is at his best where a flavor of paradox is involved, and two examples—celebrated by Father Knox as specimens of the *Sherlockismus*—are famous. As both have been misquoted in that scholarly churchman's study, it may be well to restate them from the Watsonian text. The first is a snatch of dialogue from *Silver Blaze,* the speakers being Sherlock Holmes and Inspector Gregory:

"Is there any other point to which you would wish to draw my attention?"

"To the curious incident of the dog in the night-time."

"The dog did nothing in the night-time."

"That was the curious incident," remarked Sherlock Holmes.

The second, from *The Devil's Foot,* a much later tale, is part of a conversation between the detective and a famous lion-hunter:

"You came down here to ask me whom I suspected.
. . . You then went to the vicarage, waited outside it
for some time, and finally returned to your cottage."

"How do you know that?"

"I followed you."

"I saw no one."

"That is what you may expect to see when I follow
you."

From this latter episode it is easy to see that
Holmes was not above a bit of boasting, on occasion; but it was never empty braggadocio. He knew
his powers very well, and such boasting as he in-
dulged in was usually ironic, for all its truthful-
ness. There is a flavour of Dumas in his occasional
rodomontade, a savour of D'Artagnan, who also
made no brags that he was not able and willing to
perform. And the always tacit contempt of the detective for Scotland Yard was similarly well-
grounded. His tolerant scorn of the professional
operatives is part of the very substance of the legend. Yet there is a certain apparent modesty that
accompanies his transactions. "My trifling experiences," he calls his greatest triumphs, when he
speaks of them to Watson. False modesty perhaps?
Yet not quite false, nor yet quite modest. It is
again the artist speaking, half deprecating the applause he has so well deserved. . . . "The stage,"
says Watson, "lost a fine actor, even as science lost
an acute reasoner, when he became a specialist in
crime."

It is rather obvious, also, that business lost a remarkable organizer. The number of assistants in the detective's employ—or ready to join his forces on a moment's notice—is not at any time explicitly set forth; but it must have been a large one. The ease and promptness with which a fine acting company was assembled, to play their parts outside Miss Adler's window, in *A Scandal in Bohemia*, points clearly to a highly perfected organization. And it is notorious that a veritable horde of gamins was at his call. Smart youngsters, too. "The Baker Street Division of the Detective Police Force," Holmes whimsically calls the youthful gang, upon its first appearance, in *A Study in Scarlet;* and in *The Sign of Four,* its members are the "Baker Street Irregulars." There are glimpses of them, here and there, in the *Adventures,* although their leader—a certain Wiggins—would seem to have been supplanted by a certain Simpson. It was Simpson, at any rate, who watched the rooms of Henry Wood, in Hudson Street, some months after Watson's marriage.

* * *

But Dr. Conan Doyle, in time, was weary of inventing plots. With mounting fame, the need for ready cash had passed. His program was ambitious; it even threatened the supremacy of Scott, whether or not the doctor realized it. Curiously anesthetic to the glamour of his great detective, with no faintest glimmer of a notion that he had created an immortal figure in literature and a living figure in the world, he determined that he and Holmes should part forever. The public clamour was still enormous; but Conan Doyle—the author resolutely told himself—had had enough. "I saw that I was in danger of having my hand forced, and of being entirely identified with what I regarded as a lower stratum of literary achievement." Thus his explanation, years later, when he came to write his memories. "Therefore, as a sign of my resolution, I determined to end the life of my hero."

Incredible resolution! "Murder! Murder—most foul, as in the best it is, but this most foul, strange, and unnatural."

To Dr. Conan Doyle it was natural enough, however. It was, he felt, imperative. The idea, he confessed, was in his mind when, with his wife, he visited Switzerland and saw the falls of Reichenbach. . . . "A terrible place, and one that I thought would make a worthy tomb for poor Sherlock, even if I buried my banking account along with him. So there I laid him, fully determined that he should stay there. . . ."

It is a dismaying chapter, come upon for the first time, that *Adventure of the Final Problem*. One suffers with poor Watson. "It is with a heavy heart," he says, "that I take up my pen to write these last words in which I shall ever record the singular gifts by which my friend Mr. Sherlock Holmes was distinguished." They had not seen each other in some time. The year was 1891, and Holmes presumably was in France—"engaged by the French Government upon a matter of supreme importance." It was with surprise, therefore, that Watson saw his friend walk into his consulting-room, and with consternation that he noted the detective's appearance. Sherlock Holmes was paler and more gaunt than Watson had ever seen him.

Small wonder, for he had just foiled the third of three murderous attempts upon his life, all made within the single afternoon. He was at grips, at last, with Professor Robert Moriarty, the great genius of crime. It was inevitable that they should come together at the end; and that neither one should triumph. *Moriarty!* "He is the Napoleon of crime, Watson. He is the organizer of half that is evil and of nearly all that is undetected in this great city . . . He sits motionless, like a spider in the centre of its web, but that web has a thousand radiations, and he knows well every quiver of each of them."

It was the evening of the 24th of April; that memory, at least, was burned in Watson's brain.

There was a chance, however, that Moriarty would be taken—that all would still be well. And Watson's practice, fortunately, was quiet. He was able to accompany Holmes to the Continent, whither it was certain Moriarty, if he escaped the net, would be drawn in search of them. The falls of Reichenbach were waiting their arrival. "A fearful place. . . . The long sweep of green water roaring for ever down, and the thick flickering curtain of spray hissing for ever upwards," turned Watson a bit giddy. "We stood near the edge," he says, "peering down at the gleam of the water breaking far below us against the black rocks, and listening to the half-human shout which came booming up with the spray out of the abyss." It was then the afternoon of May the 4th.

And then the false and fatal message—calling the doctor back! And Moriarty walking swiftly along the curving path that led upward to the brink! And Holmes's final letter written on torn pages from his notebook: "My dear Watson—I write these few lines through the courtesy of Mr. Moriarty, who awaits my convenience for the final discussion of those questions which lie between us. . . ."

Ah me! So they were dead, then, both of them—the great criminal and the great crime savant—deep down in the boiling depths, among the jagged rocks of Reichenbach. And Dr. Conan Doyle was free to turn his agile mind to worthier matters.

He was amazed, he tells us, at the concern expressed by the public. "You brute," began one vigorous, tearful letter of remonstrance from a woman; and from all sides were heard the sounds of lamentation. It was as if a god had been destroyed by treachery. So children mourn, perhaps, when Santa Claus is murdered by their elders.

*   *   *

The first volume of the *Adventures,* dedicated to Dr. Joseph Bell, appeared in 1892, under the imprint of George Newnes. It contained the first dozen of the twenty-four episodes, beginning with *A Scandal in Bohemia* and closing with *The Adventure of the Copper Beeches.* The second group appeared in 1894, from the same publishing house, under a slightly different title, *The Memoirs of Sherlock Holmes,* and was found to be one short of the last dozen that had appeared in the *Strand.* The adventure known as *The Cardboard Box* was omitted, the reason for omission being—it has been asserted—the author's chivalrous regret that he had allowed a woman's reputation to be smirched, a literary practice which—even fictionally—he deplored. Whatever may have been the reason, the story was resurrected and given publication, years later, between the red covers of *His Last Bow,* where it occurs most unchronologically, to raise still further doubts concerning Watson's memory.

The two tall volumes known familiarly as the *Adventures* and the *Memoirs* are to-day of considerable rarity, and are—bibliographically speaking—of the utmost desirability. Their enormous popularity in their day is evidenced by the condition in which most of them turn up. In the final chapter of copies of the *Memoirs* it is not difficult to imagine the stain of tears among the thumbprints in the margins.

Thus it was; and it was to be many years before the public knew that Sherlock Holmes was still among the living—that he was not dead, and never had been dead at all. Even Dr. Conan Doyle, himself, did not know the glorious truth. For three long years, even the devoted Watson did not know.

Good old Watson!

The Return of
Mr. Sherlock Holmes

THE late E. W. Hornung, creator of the celebrated Raffles, and brother-in-law, it is interesting to reflect, of Dr. Arthur Conan Doyle, once made a very witty remark in the form of a very bad pun. "Though he might be more humble," he observed, "there's no police like Holmes."

The public thought so, too, and the uproar that followed the supposed death of the detective, in the steaming cauldron of Reichenbach, was considerable. This was no paper hero who had gone to his death in the pages of a novel, but one of England's greatest living figures. The weeping was extensive and sincere. It is probable that the passing of no character in fiction since that of Little Nell, in Dickens's *Old Curiosity Shop*, so wrought upon the heart of England and America. But if the death of Little Nell threw nations into mourning, it should in fairness be recorded that it also wrung the heart of her creator. Conan Doyle, it must be revealed, was made of sterner stuff. . . . "I fear I was utterly callous, myself," he writes in his autobiography, "and only glad to have a chance of opening out into new fields of imagination, for the temptation of high prices made it difficult to get one's thoughts away from Holmes."

Happily, it was not only difficult; it was impossible. In spite of the success of such books as *Rodney Stone, Uncle Bernac,* and *The Tragedy of the Korosko*—admirable tales, all of them—it was Sherlock Holmes for whom the public clamored. That the great detective was dead in Switzerland, according to unimpeachable authority, made no difference, since—as it was shrewdly pointed out—there were still hundreds of his cases upon which Watson had not yet reported. They had been mentioned, time and again, in the existing chronicles. There was, for instance, the "singular tragedy of the Atkinson brothers at Trincomalee," about which the public mind had long been curious; and the "adventure of the Paradol chamber," a suggestive hint of Watson's that had not been lost upon the public imagination. More recently, there had been the "singular affair of the aluminium crutch," the "adventure of Ricoletti of the club-foot and his abominable wife," the "question of the Netherland-Sumatra Company," and other unrevealed problems in which Holmes presumably had triumphed hugely. The details of these and dozens of other cases were all in Watson's notebooks, he had testified, and the public thought it had a right to them.

When Dr. Conan Doyle at length relented, as

in time he did, it was not, however, one of the problems already mentioned by Watson that he chose to present. It was the famous *Hound of the Baskervilles,* still perhaps the most celebrated of the many adventures of Sherlock Holmes. The immortal tale began its career in the pages of the *Strand,* during 1901, and was in covers under date of the following year. It was in this same year— 1902—that Conan Doyle received his knighthood from a grateful Queen, and became Sir Arthur. Editorial gossip of the period had it that the honour was bestowed in recognition of his work in South Africa, and his history of the Boer War; but devotees of Sherlock Holmes knew better. It was a mark of royal gratitude for the return of Sherlock Holmes, one ventures, and positively nothing else.

Our own gratitude must in part be given to Mr. B. Fletcher Robinson, the author's friend, for reasons which are set forth in the dedication to the printed volume. "My dear Robinson," the notice runs, "it was to your account of a West-country legend that this tale owes its inception. For this and for your help in the details all thanks."

All thanks indeed.

*   *   *

The story is a reminiscence of the year '89, it would appear, and again Watson's memory is rather desperately at fault. In the year '89, by his own earlier figures, he was a married man, only occasionally revisiting the glimpses. It is, of course, possible that his wife was away at the time of the adventure, and that she conveniently remained away the while it ran its course; but the theory will not hold much water. At no time does he mention Mrs. Watson (née Mary Morstan), whom traditionally he married some time in 1888. To the contrary, it is clear that he and Holmes were, at the time, fellow-lodgers in Baker Street, without thought of any change. From every indication, then, the problem of the Hound preceded Watson's romantic marriage, and therefore preceded the adventure called *The Sign of Four*.

In any case, it was one of Holmes's finest problems, and Watson—good fellow—has given it to us in full. It is the longest of his many reminiscences.

The story is too well known to need retelling. Who is there that has forgotten the dreadful death of Hugo Baskerville upon the moor, and the foul, unnatural thing that stood above him? "A great black beast, shaped like a hound, yet larger than any hound that ever mortal eye has rested upon." And even as they looked upon the spectacle—the drunken roysterers who had followed—"the thing tore the throat out of Hugo Baskerville, on which, as it turned its blazing eyes and dripping jaws upon them, the three shrieked with fear and rode for dear life, still screaming, across the moor."

Two hundred years and more before, the thing

had happened; and down the years the Baskervilles had perished, father and son, by means which had been at once "sudden, bloody, and mysterious." Was it conceivable that in the nineteenth century such things were possible? Yet now Sir Charles was dead in circumstances equally mysterious and tragic.

It was a sinister affair that Dr. James Mortimer laid before the great detective, that morning in Baker Street, and one that was to pit the fathomer against a foeman worthy of his steel. The public facts were simple. No indication of violence had been discovered upon Sir Charles's person, unless it were an incredible distortion of the face. Before retiring, he had gone upon his evening walk, and never had returned alive. In the Yew Alley they had found his body, and there were evidences that he had paused beside a gate and looked out upon the moor. Organic heart disease was a sufficient explanation for the countryside. Such were the public facts. The private facts disclosed a singular circumstance which Barrymore, the butler, had neglected to relate upon the witness stand. He had said there were no traces on the ground, around the body.

But Dr. Mortimer knew better . . . "some little distance off, but fresh and clear."

"Footprints?" asked Holmes.

"Footprints."

"A man's or a woman's?"

"Mr. Holmes," the doctor whispered, "they were the footprints of a gigantic hound!"

Thus the problem opened, and that Sir Henry Baskerville did not follow Sir Charles to his ancestral doom was entirely due to Sherlock Holmes and Dr. Watson. Watson's part in the adventure is not lightly to be dismissed as unimportant. He was Holmes's surrogate at the beginning—on the scene before even the detective himself arrived; and there is Holmes's own testimony that it was an ugly and dangerous business upon which his deputy had been sent. Is there, one wonders, in all of history or fiction, an incident more thrillingly courageous than Watson's lone night charge into the empty hut upon the moor? For all he knew, the murderer was lurking just inside. And in all of the adventures there is no more taut, suspenseful moment than that which quickly follows—the moment when Watson, in a corner of the hut, hears the approaching footsteps of its occupant.

The perfect Holmes adventure, no doubt, would be a shrewd amalgam of the best parts of them all; and such a tale would of necessity include many pages from *The Hound of the Baskervilles*.

The book appeared in March of 1902, and became a classic almost overnight. The enormous popularity of Holmes, however, dictated a large first printing of the volume; in consequence of which, it is still possible, without great difficulty

HOLMES AND WATSON IN REGENT STREET
An illustration by Sidney Paget for *The Hound of
the Baskervilles.*

or expense, to obtain a copy of that first edition. Decidedly, gentlemen, it is a book to own.

But the tale was frankly from the notebooks of Dr. Watson—those capacious memorandums! It was a reminiscence of an earlier day. Poor Holmes, for all of Conan Doyle, now happily Sir Arthur, was dead and done for at the hands of Moriarty. The resurrection was a year away.

* * *

To bring the dead to life is an achievement. And Doyle had killed his hero, in *The Final Problem,* with a completeness that was appalling. Was he at all troubled in his mind about it? At the time of writing, not a whit. But it is impossible not to believe that, tardily, he knew regret. It is impossible not to feel certain that, in later years, after the murderous impulse of the moment had long passed, he wished it had been otherwise. At very least, one can imagine him as thinking, he might have left the death of Holmes in doubt. There was Arabia to which he might have sent him, instead of Switzerland. Men disappeared for years in the Arabian desert, then turned up safe and whole with manuscripts beneath their arms.

Yet the truth, when he established it, was so simple! Holmes was not dead at all. He never *had* been dead. Sir Arthur, like all the rest of us, had been mistaken; deceived by Watson's error at the brink—misled, no doubt, by Watson's later silences.

Watson, himself, had known since 1894, which was the year that "all London was interested, and the fashionable world dismayed, by the murder of the Honourable Ronald Adair, under most unusual and inexplicable circumstances." The crime was of considerable importance in itself, but it was its "inconceivable sequel" that lent it its later interest and importance to the doctor, who was by this time a widower, his wife having passed away some time during the years of Holmes's absence.

It was not to be supposed that, after the passing of his two associates, Watson would settle down with no further interest in crime; and we have his word for it that he did nothing of the sort. In point of fact, he never failed to read with care the various problems that came before the public; and more than once he even endeavored to employ the familiar methods of his mentor in their solution. For his personal satisfaction only, of course, and always —as he tells us—with indifferent success. The case of Ronald Adair, as it happened, had made a strong appeal to him; so much so that at six o'clock, one evening, he found himself one of a group of curious loafers staring up at a window in the dead man's house. Turning to leave the scene, he collided with an elderly deformed man and knocked a number of volumes from his hands.

There is no need to continue the account. The world has long since known the truth of that eventful meeting. The crippled bookman was Sherlock Holmes himself. And what more natural than his explanation, a little later, to the bewildered and delighted Watson? "My dear fellow . . . about that chasm. I had no serious difficulty in getting out of it, for the very simple reason that I was never in it."

Moriarty alone had fallen to his doom! "O frabjous day! Callooh! Callay!" One is not quoting Watson literally; but it is all there between the lines—his joy, his affection, and his satisfaction. And once more Mr. Sherlock Holmes was free to devote his life to examining "those interesting little problems which the complex life of London so plentifully presents."

For sensible reasons he had sent even Watson no word of his survival. The trial of Moriarty's sinister gang had left two of its most dangerous members at large—criminals who would leave no stone unturned to bring about the death of Holmes, once it became known that he had returned to London. Silence—a long vacation—had seemed the wisest course. For two years he had travelled in Tibet, and for a time conducted a laboratory at Montpelier, in France. Then the Park Lane Mystery had drawn him home—the murder of the Honourable Ronald Adair, which offered him peculiar personal opportunities. He was again in Baker Street, and all was as it ever had been and ever shall be.

*　　*　　*

The Return of Sherlock Holmes, a series of thirteen reminiscences in Watson's shorter manner, began to run in the *Strand Magazine* of October, 1903, and was concluded in the corresponding month of 1904. By February of 1905, the tales were in covers and another difficult volume had been added to lists of bibliophilic desiderata. The reason for the book's rarity in its first edition form, in spite of a large printing, is obviously its tremendous popularity in its day. Less difficult to find than the earliest volumes of the series, it is much scarcer than *The Hound of the Baskervilles,* which was published three years before it. That is a phenomenon that can be explained only by the supposition that the short stories are, on the whole, even more popular than the novels.

Some of the most famous of the adventures are between the covers of this book, and some of Holmes's most skilful reasoning. Few better stories are to be found in the entire saga than those, in this sixth volume, known as *The Dancing Men, The Six Napoleons,* and *The Golden Pince-nez.* It is to be noted, however, how curiously many of Holmes's problems, in essence, repeat themselves, from first to last. It is almost as if, returning after his reputed death in Switzerland, he began the cycle over again—so much in common have *A Scandal in Bohemia* and *The Norwood Builder; The Blue Carbuncle* and *The Six Napoleons; The Greek Interpreter* and *The Solitary Cyclist; The*

Naval Treaty and *The Second Stain*. And one suspects that the dangerous adventure of *The Dancing Men* followed with singular fortuity the detective's reading—or rereading—of Poe's *Gold Bug*. Not that it really matters. And, no doubt, it is merely further evidence in support of Holmes's own contention as to the way crimes duplicate each other. "There is nothing new under the sun," he told Inspector Gregson, in *A Study in Scarlet;* adding significantly: "It has all been done before."

In spite of everything, London remained a fascinating place. One can not agree with Holmes that the loss of Professor Moriarty left it a "singularly uninteresting city." And, for that matter, there was all the rest of criminal England to furnish him with problems. "From the years 1894 to 1901 inclusive, Mr. Sherlock Holmes was a very busy man," writes Watson authoritatively, at the beginning of *The Solitary Cyclist*. Not only was he consulted in all public cases of importance, but he was called upon to handle hundreds of private cases, "some of them of the most intricate and extraordinary character." Among these, few perhaps were more sensational than that involving Charles Augustus Milverton, in which Holmes and Watson committed midnight burglary to serve the ends of justice; and certainly none was more highly coloured with the hues of blood than that which saw the death of Captain Peter Carey—pinned to his cabin wall like a beetle on a card. The suggestion that Robert Moriarty had left no competent successors was surely one of Holmes's most ironic jests. Throughout this period of prolific misdemeanour the old intimacy between the two friends prevailed, and No. 221-B Baker Street again contained them both. Many were the startling quests on which they ventured forth, in fog and sunshine, and all too few of them are here in print. The fact is, at the conclusion of the *Return,* Watson is again preparing to swear off writing—or furnishing materials to Sir Arthur Conan Doyle.

It had been his intention, the doctor tells us, to conclude his series with *The Adventure of the Abbey Grange,* an oddly twisted problem that came to the collaborators one frosty morning during the winter of '97; but the circumstances of an earlier promise to relate the puzzling *Adventure of the Second Stain* obtained from Holmes a final dispensation, and for readers of 1904 a final story. Holmes, it appears, had been for some time reluctant to see the reminiscences continue. We learn the reason with somewhat of a shock. "So long as he was in actual professional practice the records of his successes were of some practical value to him; but since he has definitely retired from London and betaken himself to study and bee-farming on the Sussex Downs, notoriety has become hateful to him." Our shock is occasioned by these sudden tidings of the detective's retirement, just as we are congratulating ourselves on the fact that he is still hale and well, and back in Baker Street.

The date of publication, at this point, becomes important, however, for it enables us to establish the time of Holmes's retirement, without reference to Watson's notoriously faulty memory. It is a matter that has been a trifle cloudy; and Mr. S. C. Roberts rather begs the issue when he loosely asserts that "by 1907 Holmes had definitely retired from professional work." In point of fact, Holmes had retired by October, 1904. It was in the issue of the *Strand Magazine* of that month and year that Watson's *Second Stain* reminiscence first appeared, with its clear-cut statement revealing that the detective was even then keeping his bees upon the Sussex Downs. Precisely how long before October Holmes had given over his practice it is only possible to guess; but one ventures to think that it must have been a number of months, at least, in view of Watson's reference to his friend's objections—obviously over a period of recent time —to the "continued publication" of his experiences.

* * *

Nevertheless, three further volumes of reminiscences were to follow. Of the first, *The Valley of Fear*, published in 1914-15, it is sufficient to say that it was one of Holmes's early cases, and that it shows up Watson's memory again. Since Moriarty is the off-stage villain of the piece, not yet precipitated into Reichenbach, it is clear that the adventure belongs to a time before the working out of *The Final Problem*. Yet whereas Watson in *The Final Problem* declares his utter ignorance of even Moriarty's name, in *The Valley of Fear* he speaks of him with some familiarity. One often wonders that Holmes relied as much on Watson as he did. But the rarefied heights of Watson's unreliability —in the matter of dates—are better viewed from the opening paragraph of *Wisteria Lodge,* the first adventure in the volume known as *His Last Bow* (1917).

"I find it recorded in my notebook," he begins, "that it was a bleak and windy day towards the end of March in the year 1892. Holmes had received a telegram whilst we sat at lunch, and he had scribbled a reply. . . . Suddenly he turned upon me with a mischievous twinkle in his eyes."

But Holmes, my dear Watson, was dead beneath the falls of Reichenbach, on that bleak and windy day of March in 1892—at least, you thought he was! It was the 4th of May, in 1891, that you bent above the brink and called his name. It was not until the Spring of 1894, the year of Ronald Adair's inexplicable murder, that you met the crippled bookseller and found that he was Holmes.

But the answer is ready to our hand—even to Watson's hand. The reading is quite clear. . . . "I find it recorded in my notebook." And we have seen before that not all that went into the doctor's notebooks was beyond a suspicion of inaccuracy.

No doubt the year was 1902. If the matter is of further interest, it might be verified by a letter to the minister in London for San Pedro.

For the rest—save only for the last—the tales are apparently Watsonian reminiscences of earlier days. One, *The Bruce-Partington Plans,* is dated 1895, and is one of the finest in the saga. Written at various times between the years 1908 and 1917, they were collected from the pages of the *Strand* and issued in covers in the latter year, the year of Sherlock Holmes's ultimate service to his country. In a preface, all too brief, we have from Watson's pen the last word that has directly come to us from the Sussex Downs. "The friends of Mr. Sherlock Holmes," he writes, "will be glad to learn that he is still alive and well, though somewhat crippled by occasional attacks of rheumatism": and the detective's secret retreat is recklessly identified. He lives, it appears, "on a small farm upon the Downs, five miles from Eastbourne, where his time is divided between philosophy and agriculture."

Of Holmes's final service to his country, there is nothing now that need be said, save perhaps that —to American ears—his "Yankee" slang, throughout the adventure, is just a bit atrocious. It is as if he had just learned it all, and all at once, and was determined to omit no single word. And since, unhappily, the experience is narrated in the third person, by an unknown chronicler, no part of it may be specifically charged to Watson.

In this connection, and at this time, however, it should be said that there are scholars in the world who hold that Watson is to be charged with much more than simple inaccuracies of dating. He is the actual inventor, they assert, of certain of the adventures, which they declare to be spurious on grounds that are frequently well-taken. There are even those who insist that the final volume of the series—a set of stories put forth as *The Case-Book of Sherlock Holmes* (1927)—is so incredibly below the standard of a majority of the earlier tales as to make it highly suspect either as good Holmes or good Watson. It is a serious suggestion that they propound, and one that is involved with dangerous possibilities when it is recalled that two, at least, of the latest narratives are presumably from the pen of Holmes himself. It is an argument in which, at the moment, one prefers to take no part. Yet upon the canonicity of these dubious tales may hang no less a matter than the fact or false report of Watson's second marriage. Mr. Roberts, on the whole a fundamentalist, has been at some pains to show that Watson married—in 1902 or 1903—Miss Violet de Merville, shortly after the conclusion of *The Adventure of the Illustrious Client;* and one would like to believe him right.[1] It is, however, a theory with which one cannot agree.

And it is, of course, just possible, *n'est ce pas*, that the mind of Arthur Conan Doyle again grew

[1] S. C. Roberts: *Doctor Watson.*

weary. "I think, sir," he was told by an old Cornish boatman, whom he met, "that when Sherlock Holmes fell over that cliff, he may not have killed himself, but all the same he was never quite the same man afterwards."

Sir Arthur disagreed; and—for the most part—the rest of us are with him. Good, bad, or indifferent, one wishes that there were stories yet to come. And why may not one hope? There is still—is there not?—that long row of year-books, which filled a shelf in Baker Street; and the dispatch-cases filled with documents: "a perfect quarry for the student, not only of crime," says Watson, in *The Veiled Lodger*, but of the "social and official scandals of the late Victorian era." Sir Arthur Conan Doyle, to be sure, is dead, and Holmes has quite retired; but what of Watson?

Let us at least agree to hope that there may be made yet another attempt to destroy these damning documents. For if the outrage is repeated, we have Holmes's word to Watson, "the whole story concerning the politician, the lighthouse, and the trained cormorant will be given to the public."

No. 221-B Baker Street

ONCE upon a time—but this is not a fairy tale—
a group of French schoolboys, for reasons having
to do with scholarship or behavior, or something
of the sort, reached the English capital on a sight-
seeing tour. Asked by the erudite barker in command of their char-à-banc what they would like to
see first in London, they replied unanimously, with
a great shout, that they would like to see the lodgings of Sherlock Holmes in Baker Street. One hopes
the erudite barker was equal to the occasion.

A great many persons have felt that way about
the city of London—that Baker Street should come
before the Roman Wall and the Houses of Parliament. After all, there are shrines and shrines. And
a great many persons, during his lifetime, asked
Sir Arthur Conan Doyle to identify the house in
Baker Street. "But that is a point which for excellent reasons," he observes in his autobiography, "I
will not decide."

Has he not done so, in spite of himself?

Like the problem of what songs the sirens sang,
and what name Achilles took when he hid himself
among women, the question, although puzzling,

has not been beyond all conjecture. There is, of course, the address, which is explicitly set forth in the first sentence of the second chapter of *A Study in Scarlet;* but it is unfortunately misleading, not to say deliberately inaccurate, as tourists have discovered to their regret. It would have been impossible, however, for Sir Arthur (or for Watson) so often to have described the famous rooms without betraying some clue to their precise location, and much speculation has been pleasurably wasted upon the mystery.

"Sherlock Holmes lived on Baker Street, you will recall, hard by what is now Waterloo Station of the Underground, in that district of Georgian houses, with colorless brick fronts, little windows, iron handrails at the doors, and chimney-pots." Thus Mr. Harry Hansen, in the New York *World,* on the occasion of Sir Arthur's death. "And Baker Street," he continues, "is not very far from Piccadilly, the Strand, Trafalgar Square, and Whitehall, where the trade and politics of the seven seas were somehow unravelled and routed throughout the later nineteenth century. I myself have stood in Baker Street and surveyed a suppositious upper story, wondering whether Sherlock Holmes was standing beside the dark hangings of the windows, looking up and down for a hansom-cab with a suspicious driver. I have wondered just how Moriarty went about it to 'make the place safe,' as he called it, and pictured the streets bare of traffic and pedestrians, pervaded with a feeling of imminent danger."

But Mr. Hansen was content with the impres-

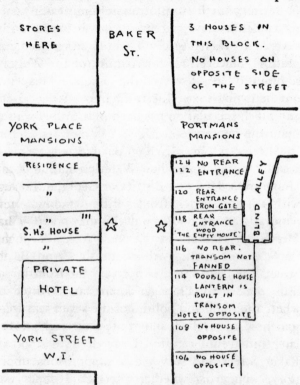

DR. BRIGGS'S MAP OF BAKER STREET.

sion, as was the present writer when he roamed the length of Baker Street upon a day in drear November. There was, indeed, a house at 66 which satisfied one's occult sense of rightness; but the notion that it was the very place has long since passed in the light of the surprising research of another quester. It required, quite plainly, the genius of another sleuth, gifted as Holmes himself was gifted, to run its eye along the many pages of the record, and find the hidden clue. All other searchers paused, then retired in confusion, when Dr. Briggs announced his solution.

The clue is in that admirable adventure of *The Empty House,* first of the collection brought together as *The Return of Sherlock Holmes.* One recalls the circumstances of that adventure, growing out of the murder of the Honourable Ronald Adair—how, after a circuitous journey through silent, menacing streets, through networks of mews and stables whose very existence to Watson had been unknown, Holmes passed at length through a wooden gate into a deserted yard, and opened the back door of the "Empty House." The description of the place is definite—almost exact. Dark as was the house within, Watson followed his companion down the long, straight hall until he dimly saw the murky fanlight over the door, in front. The window panes were thick with dust; the room was only faintly illuminated by the lamplights of the street beyond. Then Holmes's lips were at the doctor's ear.

"Do you know where we are?" he whispered.

"Surely that is Baker Street," answered the puzzled Watson, staring through the dusty window.

"Exactly. We are in Camden House, which stands opposite to our own old quarters."

Camden House!

*   *   *

Spending a part of his summer vacation in London, a few years ago, Dr. Gray Chandler Briggs of St. Louis, the well-known roentgenologist, mapped Baker Street from end to end. A labour of love—he had devoted no little of his medical leisure to a study of the text-books. One suspects that they were in his trunk and crossed the ocean with him. The *Return*, one fancies, was beneath his arm. And his kodak was in a convenient pocket. As a result of his investigations, he photographed the house at 111 and called it that of Sherlock Holmes. No more brilliant identification, one ventures, has been made in our time.

Writing of his discovery, to Frederic Dorr Steele, most famous of the detective's portraitists, the doctor set forth the minutiae of his expedition. Like Holmes himself he had approached the empty dwelling from the rear. He had turned into a narrow alley and passed through a wooden gate into a yard, to find himself at the back door which had admitted the detective. Looking in, he saw the long, straight hall extending through the house to a front door of solid wood, above which was a fan-shaped transom. Conclusive, all of it, for already over the door in front he had read the surviving placard—*Camden House.*

"There is only one house on the whole of Baker Street that answers the description," wrote the St. Louis specialist, "and when I told Sir Arthur that the sign 'Camden House' was over the door, he was amazed. He told me, with such seriousness that I could not doubt him, that he did not believe he had ever been in Baker Street in his life; if he had, it had been many years before—so long that he had forgotten! There is something spooky about Doyle, anyway," added the doctor to his friend.[1]

The deduction that followed this discovery was, obviously, elementary. Since Camden House stood opposite the famous lodgings, the rooms of Sherlock Holmes in Baker Street were, of necessity, those upon the second story of the building numbered 111. One wonders if the doctor counted the steps. There were seventeen, you will recall, leading upward from the lower hall to the collaborators' sitting-room. Watson was ragged a bit about them, in the opening pages of *A Scandal in Bohemia*. But there was no bay window, noted Dr. Briggs, Watson to the contrary notwithstanding. That, he supposed, was one of his famous confrère's little fictions.[2]

* * *

[1] F. D. Steele: *Sherlock Holmes*.
[2] Mr. H. W. Bell, in his *Sherlock Holmes and Dr. Watson*, takes serious issue with Dr. Briggs, pointing out that the northernmost portion of the present Baker Street, including the building at 111, was, until January 1, 1921, known as York Place. Throughout the entire active career of Sherlock Holmes,

For every reader there is, no doubt, a different picture of that famous living-room. And probably it is not subject to change. Do you prefer it on a blazing day in August, when "Baker Street was like an oven, and the glare of the sunlight upon the yellow brickwork of the house across the road was painful to the eye"? A day when "it was hard to believe that these were the same walls which loomed so gloomily through the fogs of winter"? On one such day, at least, with all the blinds half drawn, Holmes lay upon the sofa and read a letter that he had received by the morning post, which was to call him to the adventure of *The Cardboard Box.* But Watson's term of service in India, he tells us, had trained him to stand the heat better than the cold; a thermometer at 90 was no hardship for the veteran Watson.

Or do you like an evening of late September, when the equinoctial gales are raging with exceptional violence? Such days and nights brought tragic cases to the sitting-room in Baker Street. What a picture, for instance, is recorded by Watson in those early pages of *The Five Orange Pips!*

"All day the wind had screamed and the rain had beaten against the windows, so that even here

---

he sets forth, the building at 111 was known as No. 30, York Place, a circumstance which he believes invalidates the doctor's identification, in spite of the striking clue offered by Camden House. This problem is still in debate, and offers material for as notable a mystery as the present whereabouts of the vanished head of Cromwell.

in the heart of great hand-made London we were forced to raise our minds for the instant from the routine of life, and to recognize the presence of those great elemental forces which shriek at mankind through the bars of his civilization, like untamed beasts in a cage. As evening drew in the storm grew louder and louder, and the wind cried and sobbed like a child in the chimney. Sherlock Holmes sat moodily at one side of the fireplace cross-indexing his records of crime, whilst I at the other was deep in one of Clark Russell's fine sea stories, until the howl of the gale from without seemed to blend with the text, and the splash of the rain to lengthen out into the long swash of the sea waves."

And then, the bell—inevitably the bell.

Looking from the window on such a night, which was a habit with both Holmes and Watson, one might have seen the occasional lamps gleaming on the expanse of muddy road and shining pavement, and perhaps "a single cab . . . splashing its way from the Oxford Street end" to deposit Inspector Stanley Hopkins on the detective's doorstep. And not always on such tempestuous evenings did Holmes attack his files with moody industry, nor Watson lose himself at sea. There were times when they sat together in busy silence all the evening, the detective perhaps "engaged with a powerful lens deciphering the remains of the original inscription upon a palimpsest," and Watson "deep in a recent treatise upon surgery." Sooner or later, however, they were called away. It is at least astonishing, the number of cases that came to Holmes and Watson in inclement season, dragging them from their comfortable hearth to brave the rigours of indecent English weather.

Or will you have a cold morning in the early Spring, with thick fog rolling down between the lines of dun-colored houses, and the opposing windows looming "like dark, shapeless blurs through the heavy yellow wreaths"? The gas is lighted and shines upon the white tablecloth, and upon the glimmer of china and metal, and upon Sherlock Holmes and Dr. Watson at breakfast, on either side of a cheery fire, in the old room in Baker Street. Emerging from a cloud of newspapers, in which he has been reading the agony columns, the detective lights his long cherrywood pipe with a glowing cinder lifted from the coals, and lectures Watson upon the sensationalism of his records.

Not that they always breakfasted together. A schedule of their appearances at table would be valuable and interesting, but unfortunately impossible. It all depended. That Holmes rose late we have been several times assured—save, to be sure, on those occasions when he was up all night—yet there were times when Watson breakfasted after Holmes. The record is surprisingly confused, and the only possible inference is—as Father Knox points out— that Watson breakfasted very late indeed. His own assertion that he was regular in his habits has little bearing on the matter. He may have risen at noon and still have been quite regular. Certain it is that he resented early calls. Holmes, to the contrary, took what sleep he could, and occasionally stayed in bed for several days. But one likes to find them breakfasting together, and wishes that it might have happened oftener. Rashers of bacon seem to have been a staple, with sometimes eggs and always toast and coffee.

*   *   *

But attractive as is the picture of Holmes and Watson at their ease, it must be reiterated that it is a picture touched with some confusion. Precisely where to place the chairs and tables, for example, the sofas and the shelves of books, and all the other dear impedimenta of the sitting-room, is somewhat of a problem. Holmes, for all his orderly methods of thought, was notoriously untidy in many of his personal habits. One suspects that he moved things round to meet the exigencies of the moment, and left them much as he had finished with them. One fancies Watson following in his track and putting things to rights again. But, generally, one thinks, the life of the detective went on around the fireplace. It follows then that everything he might require would be within his reach; certainly it would be so by evening, on any day that he remained at home.

Not that Watson was conventional. "The rough-

and-tumble work in Afghanistan," he tells us, "coming on top of a natural Bohemianism of disposition," had made him rather more lax than befitted a medical man. But there was a limit, even for Watson. "When I find a man," he asserts, "who keeps his cigars in the coal scuttle, his tobacco in the toe-end of a Persian slipper, and his unanswered correspondence transfixed by a jackknife into the very centre of his wooden mantelpiece, then I begin to give myself virtuous airs. I have always held, too," he adds, "that pistol practice should distinctly be an open-air pastime; and when Holmes in one of his queer humours would sit in an arm-chair, with his hair-trigger and a hundred Boxer cartridges, and proceed to adorn the opposite wall with a patriotic V.R. done in bullet-pocks, I felt strongly that neither the atmosphere nor the appearance of our room was improved by it."

In these early paragraphs of *The Musgrave Ritual,* we have perhaps our most illuminating description of the room's untidiness. That it was not always so, later expressions would seem to indicate; it may be that Holmes, as time went on, improved. But "our chambers," Watson says, "were always full of chemicals and of criminal relics, which had a way of wandering into unlikely positions, and of turning up in the butter-dish, or in even less desirable places." It was his friend's papers, however, that principally distressed the doctor; they were all over the place. "He had a horror of destroying documents, especially those which were connected with his past cases, and yet it was only once in every year or two that he would muster energy to docket and arrange them. . . . Thus month after month his papers accumulated, until every corner of the room was stacked with bundles of manuscript which were on no account to be burned, and which could not be put away save by their owner."

There can be little doubt that Watson was a very patient man. One suspects that there were protests, now and then, that have been omitted from the record. No doubt he rushed into the street when, as occasionally happened, the room became too malodorously a laboratory. The detective's chemical investigations went forward, it would appear, at a side-table. Pictures of this side of his activity occur from time to time, and one is afforded by the opening pages of *The Naval Treaty* that is memorable.

"A large curved retort was boiling furiously in the bluish flame of a Bunsen burner, and the distilled drops were condensing into a two-litre measure. . . . He dipped into this bottle or that, drawing out a few drops of each with his glass pipette, and finally brought a test-tube containing a solution over to the table. In his right hand he had a slip of litmus-paper."

It is another of those unforgettable vignettes of the detective and the doctor in their rooms in

Baker Street. If the paper remained blue, then all was well. If it turned red, it meant "the life of a man." Holmes dipped the paper into the test-tube, and it flushed at once into a dull and dirty crimson. . . .

"I shall be at your service in one instant, Watson," said Sherlock Holmes, looking up from his labors. "You will find the tobacco in the Persian slipper."

O memorable and thrilling moment that still contrives to stir the happy reader, even upon a thirty-first perusal!

* * *

It is one of the landmarks, by the way—that Persian slipper. One fancies that it hung upon the wall and not too far from Holmes's arm-chair near the fireplace. Opposite the detective's chair would be the doctor's—an arm-chair also, we are told—and it is likely that they seldom interchanged. Holmes's was low and worn, and obviously it was broad enough to contain the coiled length of the detective in his moments of profoundest concentration. The other chairs were scattered anywhere, one thinks, and three at least are indicated—a wooden chair, a cane-backed chair occasionally occupied by Watson, and another arm-chair, presumably for guests. There was also a settee and, just possibly, a pair of sofas; or it may be that when Watson spoke of sofas he was thinking of a sofa

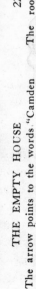

THE EMPTY HOUSE

The arrow points to the words "Camden House" on the sign over the door.

221-B, BAKER STREET

The rooms of Sherlock Holmes and Dr. Watson, as discovered by Dr. Briggs.

and a settee. Certainly there was a lamp—in addition to the conventional gas fixtures of the period —and this would stand upon the principal table, beside the breakfast bell: and between the table and the hearth there stretched the bearskin rug. Who has forgotten the extraordinary entrance of Dr. Thorneycroft Huxtable, M.A., Ph.D., etc., whose first action when the door had closed was to stagger against the table and then collapse upon the hearth-rug?

In a corner, when it was not in use, stood the acid-stained deal-top chemical table, with its accompanying stool. Was there also a bench, one wonders; or was it bench and table according to the moment's whim? In another corner leaned the violin case; and somewhere stood a pipe-rack filled with pipes. The spirit-case and gasogene, one thinks, were in the corner with the violin, and probably upon a shelf; one of the shelves, no doubt, that held the detective's books. Precisely where to set the desks down, though, is a puzzle. There were two of them, one Holmes's and one Watson's; and what with a safe still waiting to be placed, the room begins to seem a bit congested. Conceivably the safe was in the detective's bedroom.

The mantel, one gathers, was a mess. The clock stood there; and all of Holmes's unanswered correspondence, as we have seen, was transfixed in its centre by the detective's knife: but that it held still other cluttering matters is easily imaginable. For example, loose tobacco. Watson is clear upon the point. Calling upon his friend, in the early pages of the case of Mr. Victor Hatherley, he found the fathomer smoking his early morning pipe, while waiting for his breakfast—a "before-breakfast pipe," the doctor tells us, "which was composed of all the plugs and dottles left from his smokes of the day before, all carefully dried and collected on the corner of the mantelpiece." And certainly there would be also books and pipes and glasses.

On the walls one visualizes the scientific charts and such pictures as the collaborators found alluring. A queer conglomeration! Two of Watson's are of record—a portrait of General Gordon, framed, and an unframed portrait of the American Beecher. That the latter ultimately acquired a frame and found its place upon the walls seems more than likely in view of Watson's thought of it. For a time, however, it merely stood on top of the doctor's books, a circumstance which permits us to deduce that the friends made shift to keep their books apart. And the books, no doubt, were in their shelves against the wall. The doctor's taste in literature was not exactly notable, but we may assume a medical collection of some merit, with here and there, perhaps, one of Clark Russell's fine sea stories and a yellow-backed novel of a sensational and inexpensive sort.

The library of Sherlock Holmes, if one may call it that, was personal and proprietary, but decently eclectic. It would be a pleasant task to catalogue it for the record; but that one would be justified in placing upon the shelves each writer ever quoted by the detective, is subject for debate. Of Holmes's reading we are given many glimpses in the long series of his adventures. It is a very respectable list of authors; and this in spite of Watson's early libel that his companion's knowledge of literature and philosophy was *nil*. A man who is able to compare Hafiz with Horace, and to quote Tacitus and Thoreau, Jean Paul, Flaubert, and Goethe, aptly and without hesitation, is not a man who may be lightly called unread. Carlyle and Meredith, too, figure in the detective's reading; they may even have been upon his shelves—and we may be rather sure of Winwood Reade. One suspects a Bible, somewhere on the premises. But we may be entirely certain only of the reference works; they were there, unquestionably, in number, from the current *Whitaker* to the red line of *Baedekers,* and biographical encyclopaedias without end. Foremost, however, on the shelves, in any list, must always stand that row of formidable scrapbooks—the detective's own —which so many of his fellow citizens would have been happy to destroy.[1]

"For many years," says Watson, "he had adopted a system of docketing all paragraphs concerning men and things, so that it was difficult to name a

[1] The library of books on crime and criminals collected by Sir Arthur Conan Doyle was purchased by Dr. A. S. W. Rosenbach—for his own collection—after the novelist's death.

subject or a person on which he could not at once furnish information." One sees them stretched across a section of the room, all neatly lettered on their buckram backs in the precise and clerkly hand of Sherlock Holmes.

Somehow one doubts that Holmes or Watson ran to bookplates.

* * *

There were two bedrooms in the place, as we know from Watson's earliest record; about the doctor's we have the scantiest possible information. He comes from it, he goes into it; and there the record ends. One assumes, of course, a bed.

Of Holmes's private chamber there is a clear description. Since there was a blind, which Watson was once warned to leave alone, there was perforce a window; it looked upon the street. No other arrangement is remotely possible, in view of statements in *The Mazarin Stone*. There was a bed and possibly a safe; and certainly there was a mantel, which indicates, no doubt, a minor fireplace. The mantel, like that within the sitting-room, was a holy mess. "A litter of pipes, tobacco-pouches, syringes, pen-knives, revolver cartridges, and other *débris* was scattered over it." And every wall was covered with the portraits of celebrated criminals.

Three rooms comprised the suite; the arrangement, one takes it, was the simplest one: that is, the three were on a line, the famous sitting-room between the bedrooms, and each looked into Baker Street. Inexpensive as they were, to begin with— when Holmes and Watson first engaged them—it would appear that they advanced in price as time went on. One fancies Holmes's generosity to have been as much responsible as any pressure brought by Mrs. Hudson. "The atmosphere of violence and danger which hung around him," as Watson says, unquestionably made him as undesirable a tenant as might be found in London. Realizing this, it is quite possible that the detective increased his rental of his own volition. Certain it is, at any rate, that within a few years of his assuming occupancy —when, indeed, he was living in the rooms alone, Watson having married and gone domestic ways— his payments had become "princely." And Watson had no doubt that the house might have been purchased at the price which Holmes paid for the rooms during the years they were together.

The point inevitably raises the question of the detective's profits, and the suggestion is that they were enormous. Yet in the face of this we have the assertion of Holmes himself that he is—or was—a poor man. The facts would seem to lie somewhere between the two extremes; and it is, of course, to be remembered that poverty and wealth are relative terms. "My professional charges are upon a fixed scale," Holmes coldly told the American Gold King, Gibson, for whom he undertook the problem of *Thor Bridge*. "I do not vary them, save when I remit them altogether." But this was simply an assertion of great dignity in the face of a client whom he did not like. Fundamentally true as no doubt it was, it took no heed of great rewards offered in behalf of more reputable endeavours. The truth is, one suspects, Holmes was a bit of a Robin Hood where money was concerned; that is, he scrupled not to take large sums where clients could afford it. Certainly he balanced the account by handling many cases without charge at all. And what seemed "princely" to the humble Watson— in the matter of Holmes's rental—may after all have been no more than decent.

*   *   *

Thus, then, one sees the rooms in Baker Street, and somewhere on the premises a dressing gown. Within the dressing gown is Sherlock Holmes. One does not hold with Father Knox that Watson, in this connection, was inconsistent—because the famous gown, early described as blue, was later called by other shades and colours, to the bewilderment of careful readers. It is nowhere explicitly asserted, reverend sir, that Mr. Sherlock Holmes possessed a single robe and that of stated hue. To the contrary, the constant inference is that there were several. That the doctor has shown us his friend and hero in robes of different colours is evidence, if anything, of accuracy. In a London practice covering more than a score of years, a dozen dressing gowns may well be indicated.

And Watson, too, is there within the room, as much a fixture as the detective himself. That solid, English figure—"a middle-sized, strongly built man; square jaw, thick neck, moustache"—must be forever the second figure in the immemorial tableau; a man with qualities of heart and mind that command our love even when we laugh most loudly at his stupidities. His independent virtues are not clamorous; but of the two collaborators he would be the least trying upon a desert island. It is through the eyes of this dull, good fellow that we behold the greater figure of his more celebrated companion. It is his devotion to his friend that is, in large degree, responsible for ours.

And Mrs. Hudson? She too is on the scene, whenever she is needed—sometimes when she is not. Once, alas, she was called Turner—Mrs. Turner. It was during the preliminary excitements of the case of Irene Adler, when Watson's marriage had kept the friends apart; but it is inconceivable that the doctor should have forgotten her name. His mind, no doubt, was on some other matter at the moment, as he set down the record of that curious episode. A patient whose name was Turner was, no doubt, awaiting his attention. Mrs. Hudson, landlady at No. 221-B Baker Street, is Mrs. Hudson—and nobody else in the world.

Thus they lived; and thus they live—and the old

building is there, says Dr. Briggs, to prove it. Sherlock Holmes and Baker Street! It was no idle anecdote, that story of the char-à-banc of schoolboys.

And who is Sherlock Holmes? The spirit of a town and of a time. He is the fog, says William Bolitho, "in that crying old street, Baker Street; the glow of sea coal in the grates, where the English servant brings in to you tea and muffins, and snug napkins of odorous toast. He is . . . the mystery of the house opposite; of the grubby little shop around the corner you noticed and wondered about; of the old, old lady, half perceived in her shining brougham, who passes through empty Eaton Square every Wednesday afternoon. Sherlock is he who answers when you ask the air, Who lives there, I wonder? What is the story behind that drawn blind in London? . . . From him you may expect something much too subtle to be advertised. Cabs slurring through the mud, sounds and sights and presences of the old nineties in Baker Street—that time and that place which above all thought itself final, and that nothing different was ever going to happen again." [1]

[1] William Bolitho: *The Last Bow.*

The Private Life of
Mr. Sherlock Holmes

IT IS, of course, notorious—we have Watson's word
for it—that Mr. Sherlock Holmes "loathed every
form of society with his whole Bohemian soul."
The word *society* is poorly chosen. What Watson—
a careless writer—intended to convey was that *social
life* offended the Bohemian soul of his companion;
in consequence of which emotion he preferred to
spend his time in Baker Street when others might
have gone to teas and parties: "buried among his
old books," as Watson says, "and alternating from
week to week between cocaine and ambition—the
drowsiness of the drug and the fierce energy of his
own keen nature."

In time, it is true, the doctor weaned him from
the drug—to the detriment of romantic interest,
whatever the benefit to Holmes—but even then it
is seldom that one finds the saturnine detective ac-
cepting or turning down an invitation. He simply
didn't get them. No doubt there had been plenty
of them in his youth; but in the face of his consist-
ent declinations—after an experience or two, perhaps, with bores—he would in time, of course, be

let alone. It is, one fancies, almost as great a nuisance to be a detective as to be a doctor: there are always guests with problems to present.

The fact is, Watson too preferred the silences or the friendly arguments of Baker Street to any attraction London had to offer—a circumstance in which he is at one with his adoring readers. Each man preferred the company of the other, and was glad enough, no doubt, even to see a client leave the doorstep. Even, perhaps, Lestrade or Tobias Gregson. Even, perhaps, Inspector Stanley Hopkins; although for Hopkins Holmes had a considerable admiration, and on a cold night a prescription containing whisky.

To the casual student of the detective's cases it may appear that the rooms in Baker Street were always crowded. His first impression may be that of a bewildered client teetering on the rug; an arm-chair in which the detective is curled like a Mohammedan, smoking shag; a cane-backed chair or sofa containing Watson; and Mrs. Hudson entering to announce Lestrade—whose footstep is on the stair. In actuality, there were long hours of comradely communion between the occupants. Seldom indeed did anyone stay the night. And some of the happiest memories, surely, of the epic history are those of Holmes and Watson living their simple, private lives. Not Crusoe and his admirable Friday—one had almost said his goat—were more resolutely at home upon their island than Sherlock Holmes and

Watson in their living-room. They passed there some of the most felicitous moments of their common life.

Not that they did not, on occasion, venture the Victorian whirl. There is ample record that Holmes, at least, was fond of opera—sufficiently so to hurry to Covent Garden, on a Wagner night, with no hope of arriving before the second act. This was after the successful culmination of the *Red Circle* adventure, and was possibly in the nature of a reward. Similarly, it will be remembered, after some weeks of severe work on the problem presented by Sir Henry Baskerville, the pair went off to hear the De Reszkes in *Les Huguenots*. Holmes had procured a box, and on the way they stopped at Marcini's for a little dinner. "Turning their thoughts into more pleasant channels," was the way in which Holmes described the De Reszke adventure. A musician himself, he would naturally turn to music for rest and surcease, after a desperate morning round with murderers. Not always was his own violin sufficient.

As early in their association as the celebrated *Study in Scarlet* the detective had dragged his companion off to Hallé's concert, after a triumphant morning of detection at Lauriston Gardens. Neruda was to play: "Her attack and her bowing are splendid," commented Sherlock Holmes. "What's that little thing of Chopin's she plays so magnificently?" If he really expected Watson to answer him, the suggestion is clear that the doctor also knew something about music. And luncheon, of course, immediately preceded Neruda. Both men, without being gluttons, were fond of eating, and frequently they posted off to some favourite London restaurant. After the hideous comedy of the *Dying Detective* it was to Simpson's they went for sustenance, however; not Marcini's. Possibly it seemed a better place to eat when food in quantity was what was needed. Holmes, it will be recalled, had been at that time fasting for several days.

*　　*　　*

St. James's Hall was also a favourite sanctuary when it was possible for Holmes to interrupt his sleuthing. "And now, Doctor, we've done our work; it's time we had some play," one hears him cry to Watson, after a brilliant morning of deduction. "A sandwich and a cup of coffee; then off to violin land, where all is sweetness and delicacy and harmony, and there are no red-headed clients to vex us with their conundrums." The occasion of this pleasant interlude was the intermission, as it were, before the "crash" in the fantastic problem of Mr. Jabez Wilson. And all that afternoon, the doctor tells us, "he sat in the stalls, wrapped in the most perfect happiness, gently waving his long thin fingers in time to the music"—listening to Sarasate play the violin.

The picture galleries, too, it must be assumed,

were browsing-spots attractive to the collaborators. No doubt they served as stop-gaps in the long days of criminal investigation—when it was possible pleasantly to while away an hour while waiting for an appointment. A clue to this diversion is to be found in the early pages of the *Hound;* after the profitable discovery of the bearded man, in Regent Street: "And now, Watson, it only remains for us to find out by wire the identity of the cabman . . . and then we will drop into one of the Bond Street picture-galleries and fill in the time until we are due at the hotel." But the incident was not, we may be sure, an isolated one. The mind turns easily at such times to the familiar groove. Did they, one wonders, care for Mr. Whistler? Or was "The Charge of the Scots Greys" more to their British taste?

It is quite clear, at any rate, that the occasional social exercises of the two were largely cultural. When they went forth from Baker Street, it was upon a trail of evil import or to a place of decent entertainment. Occasionally, to a Turkish bath; and very likely—one suspects—now and again to Madame Tussaud's. On the whole, however, they preferred to stay at home. Away from it, the detective's temper was always uncertain, Watson tells us: "Without his scrapbooks, his chemicals, and his homely untidiness, he was an uncomfortable man."

From time to time they travelled on the continent, not always on the business of a client; and several parts of rural England knew them well. It was on one of these joint vacation jaunts that they chanced upon the ugly business of the *Reigate Squires*—when they were the guests of Colonel Hayter, down in Surrey; and it was presumably a holiday adventure of a sort that furnished them the instructive problem of the *Three Students*—a sort of pendant to Holmes's laborious researches into early English charters. Again, it was a vacation trip that took them—in 1897—to the small cottage near Poldhu Bay, at the further extremity of the Cornish peninsula, in which singular and sinister neighborhood there befell that gruesome experience chronicled by Watson as *The Devil's Foot*. Once, it is certain, they went to Norway; but if aught of criminal interest developed during the visit, it has yet to be reported.

From these vacation trips—interrupted as they invariably were by theft or murder—Holmes always returned to Baker Street refreshed. It was, however, only the thefts and murders that consoled him for the time thus spent away from Baker Street.

And it is at home, in Baker Street, that one likes best to think of them—alone and puttering with their secret interests. Little vignettes of perfect happiness, wreathed in tobacco smoke and London fog.

Of course they took in all the daily papers, and

read them with a diligence almost incredible. Did the detective prop his journal against the breakfast sugar bowl? And did Watson, when he sat down at table, invariably thump his knee against the leg? For Watson, at any rate, there was usually a lecture. . . . After the return from Switzerland— by way of Lhassa—the papers rather disappointed Holmes. With Moriarty dead, London, from the point of view of the criminal expert, he said, had become a singularly uninteresting city. . . . "With that man in the field one's morning paper presented infinite possibilities. Often it was only the smallest trace, Watson, the faintest indication, and yet it was enough to tell me that the great malignant brain was there, as the gentlest tremors of the edges of the web remind one of the foul spider which lurks in the centre. Petty thefts, wanton assaults, purposeless outrage—to the man who held the clue all could be worked into one connected whole. To the scientific student of the higher criminal world no capital of Europe offered the advantages which London then possessed. But now——!"

One sees the pile of papers growing in a corner, mounting up toward the gasogene and pipe-rack, till in a fit of energy Holmes scissored them to fragments. That rid the room of papers, for the nonce, but presented the new problem of the clippings: there were probably thousands waiting to be pasted up. And then, another night, another burst of energy, and some hundreds would at length be docketed. Over the years the row of scrapbooks lengthened on the shelf. Cold winter evenings or rainy nights of autumn were likely to be dedicated to the pasting-up; sometimes to indexing what already had been pasted. A never-ending chore. When and if ever the British Museum shall acquire the scrapbooks of Mr. Sherlock Holmes one hopes to read the volume under V—a fascinating miscellany. The *Voyage* of the "Gloria Scott" is there, and a biography of *Victor Lynch* the forger. Also the case of *Vanderbilt* and the Yeggman—unchronicled by Watson—and somewhat concerning *Vittoria* the circus belle. *Vigor,* the Hammersmith Wonder, too; and *Vipers*—possibly *Vodka*—and a Draculian paper about *Vampires.* . . .

Holmes obviously had a system of his own. Most scrapbook makers would simply have listed *Lynch* and *lizard* under the letter L, letting it go at that. But the detective indexed his clippings to the last adjective and adverb.

* * *

The relationship between the collaborators was ideal, after the years had taught them to know each other. About his own share in the partnership Watson had no illusions; but he was not too servile. Some thousands of his readers, he must have known, would happily have traded places with him. His statement as to himself and Sherlock Holmes, candidly prefixed to the adventure of the *Creeping*

Man, is admirably lucid and not a little penetrating: "The relations between us," he asserts, "were peculiar. He was a man of habits, narrow and concentrated habits, and I had become one of them. As an institution I was like the violin, the shag tobacco, the old black pipe, the index books, and others perhaps less excusable. When it was a case of active work and a comrade was needed upon whose nerve he could place some reliance, my rôle was obvious. But apart from this I had uses. I was a whetstone for his mind, I stimulated him. He liked to think aloud in my presence. His remarks could hardly be said to be made to me—many of them would have been as appropriately addressed to his bedstead—but none the less, having formed the habit, it had become in some way helpful that I should register and interject. If I irritated him by a certain methodical slowness in my mentality, that irritation served only to make his own flame-like intuitions and impressions flash up the more vividly and swiftly. Such was my humble rôle in our alliance."

During the day, when no active occupation offered, Holmes smoked his pipe and meditated. With a case on hand, he also smoked and meditated. Sometimes—the picture is famous—he would sit for hours "curled up in the recesses of his shabby chair." Sometimes, in search of information, he "sat upon the floor like some strange Buddha, with crossed legs, the huge books all around him, and one open upon his knees." Obviously, the nature of the problem offered for his solution had an important bearing on his habits. Sometimes "a formidable array of bottles and test-tubes, with the pungent cleanly smell of hydrochloric acid" would tell the doctor—hastening in, himself, after a session with his patients—that he had "spent his day in the chemical work which was so dear to him." Sometimes, horizontal upon a couch, wrapped in a purple gown—"a pipe-rack within his reach upon the right, and a pile of crumpled morning papers . . . near at hand"—the doctor would discover him in rapt examination of a hat which was for the moment an intellectual problem.

There is a curious glamour in the most trivial passages between the two, a sense of significance—of impending revelation—perhaps not always justified by the detective's disclosure. It is part of Watson's charm that he sets down everything. One would not have it otherwise. The little triumphs that are no part or parcel of the tale are his habitual prolegomena; they are our glimpses of that private life they lived together, when only the reader's eye might spy them out. . . .

"Sherlock Holmes," one genuinely thrills to hear, "had been bending for a long time over a low-power microscope. Now he straightened himself up and looked round at me in triumph. 'It is glue, Watson,' said he. 'Unquestionably it is glue. Have a look at these scattered objects in the field!' "

Actively engaged upon a malodorous bit of brewing, "his long, thin back curved over a chemical vessel" and his head sunk upon his chest, the detective looked to Watson "like a strange, lank bird, with dull grey plumage and a black top-knot." There is no need to illustrate the scene. But this would be, of course, upon a day when Holmes had put on his dressing-gown of grey, instead of the more familiar purple horror. On the whole, the picture that Watson has most vividly conveyed is that of Holmes recumbent—languid yet somehow rigid in his chair, wreathed in the vapours from his favourite pipe. The favourite pipe, of course, being subject always to change; since nothing, as Holmes himself remarked, has more individuality than a pipe, "save perhaps watches and bootlaces." For every mood in Baker Street there was a pipe. One sees him still as Watson saw and described him in that last of all the series of adventures. . . . "Holmes lay with his gaunt figure stretched in his deep chair, his pipe curling forth slow wreaths of acrid tobacco, while his eyelids drooped over his eyes so lazily that he might almost have been asleep were it not that at any halt or questionable passage of my narrative they half lifted, and two grey eyes, as bright and keen as rapiers, transfixed me with their searching glance."

One notes with interest that Holmes's eyes were grey. It is the only record of their colour.

* * *

Occasionally, when the day was really fine, the friends walked in the streets, savouring the singular sights and sounds of London. Shop windows were of interest to them both, and passers-by absorbing. "The park"—some park or other—was close at hand, and it is of record that they sometimes strolled there. Watson's account of one such episode is subdued. . . . "The first faint shoots of green were breaking out upon the elms, and the sticky spearheads of the chestnuts were just beginning to burst into their five-fold leaves. For two hours we rambled about together, in silence for the most part, as befits two men who know each other intimately." But this diversion was not customary, since it encroached on office hours. And on the afternoon described they missed a client. "There had been a gentlemen asking for them."

"Holmes glanced reproachfully at me," confesses Watson. " 'So much for afternoon walks!' said he."

The afternoons then were spent in running down their cases—the detective's cases—not often strolling in the park. And for all his love of Baker Street, it may be noted, during the active progress of a case Holmes was quite capable of hiding out. It is an interesting revelation, frequently overlooked, that Watson makes in his account of the adventure called *Black Peter*. . . . "He had at least five small refuges in different parts of London in which he was able to change his personality." The reference is tantalizing and obscure. The rooms of

SCOTLAND YARD

ENTRANCE TO THE "YARD"

THE WIGMORE STREET POST OFFICE
Where Watson got red mud on his shoes.

Mycroft Holmes, opposite the Diogenes Club, would certainly be one of them; but it would be satisfying to know the others. At such times—when he was operating in disguise—Holmes sometimes took the name of "Captain Basil," the better to deceive his casual assistants and to deceive and confound his unsuspecting enemies. It may be assumed that in all of his five refuges he stored the materials of deception, as well as quantities of shag tobacco.

Not all of the detective's cases, though, drove him to his retreats or to his arm-chair. Sometimes for hours—once, certainly, for a whole day—he rambled about the living-room with knotted brows, his head upon his breast, charging and recharging his strongest pipe, and deaf to all of Watson's questionings. These were his bad days, when the trail was faint, and even Watson had failed him as a whetstone.

But it was to the papers that both invariably returned. The everlasting, never-ceasing papers. Edition after edition of them was delivered at the rooms, probably by the stout and puffing Mrs. Hudson, who would have them from the urchin at the door. Not only Holmes but Watson saturated himself with the unending chronicle of news; and they read it—it must be admitted—with a surprisingly reckless acceptance of its accuracy. In America, Holmes would have taken *none* of the papers in. In America, the papers are for the credulous Watsons.

It is at night one likes them best perhaps—the curious companions. And preferably with a beating rain outside. If Stanley Hopkins has dropped in from Scotland Yard, no matter; their simple hospitality is as hearty as it is restrained and masculine. They did not always save the whisky for Stanley Hopkins. Themselves, occasionally, good fellows, they tippled companionably. And usually in the early morning hours, after a trying day with thug or cracksman. Whisky-and-soda and a bit of lemon. And all the credit gone to Scotland Yard. Midnight or very early in the morning—the time of relaxation and revelation, while the "undying flame" leaps on the hearth. Holmes lifts out a glowing cinder with the tongs; lights the long pipe of sprightly disputation. "You see, Watson," he patiently begins, "it was all perfectly obvious from the first. . . ."

In the long evenings, too, Holmes played his fiddle. Doubtless his bowing was not comparable to Neruda's, but it was good enough for Watson. "Sometimes the chords were sonorous and melancholy. Occasionally they were fantastic and cheerful. Clearly they reflected the thoughts which possessed him, but whether the music aided those thoughts, or whether the playing was simply the result of a whim or fancy," was more than Watson could determine. And when some haunting strain had charmed and soothed the doctor—moved him to ask the name of the composer—as like as not it would be something by Sherlock Holmes.

* * *

Then, of an evening in the depths of February, one fancies Watson questing another tale. Permission, perhaps, to reveal an untold problem—one of the many hinted and then withheld. The truth, perhaps, about the atrocious conduct of Colonel Upwood, or the peculiar persecution of John Vincent Harden. It is understandable that some reticence must be observed with reference to the sudden death of Cardinal Tosca—an investigation carried out at the personal request of His Holiness, the Pope—and in that delicate matter arranged by Holmes for the reigning family of Holland; but surely the time must be at hand, thinks Watson, for the full disclosure of facts in the Tankerville Club Scandal. That often he spoke of these to Holmes, there can be no doubt at all. Having half promised his readers that he would some day tell them, his position may well have seemed to him embarrassing.

One sympathizes heartily with Watson. Too long has the world awaited the adventure of the Amateur Mendicant Society—which held a luxurious club in the lower vault of a furniture warehouse—and the little problem of the Grosvenor Square Furniture Van. The case of Wilson, the Notorious

Canary-Trainer, too, is a whisper full of fascinating suggestion; and one would give much to read the long-suppressed adventure of the Tired Captain.

Holmes, we may be certain, listened to some urgent argument on evenings when the doctor decided to consider his reading public. Frequently he chided the narrator for his literary shortcomings, pretending that the tales were sad affairs; but when he came to write just two of them, himself, he changed his tune.

One can imagine them in whimsical discussion of the *ifs* of their achievements—the *what ifs,* as it were, conducted *post mortem* upon their cases. As for instance, after the rocket-throwing episode in the amusing case of Irene Adler. It is impossible to read the tale without a bit of wonderment: what if the ingenious rocket had missed fire? Would not the whole planned sequence have gone agley? But Watson, although he may have faltered, never actually blundered. Holmes knew the qualities of his assistant. No case was ever lost by Watson's failure. And his reward—all that he ever asked or cared for—was an approving word or nod from Holmes. Did not he get them both, outside the record? During those nights in Baker Street, perhaps? After the problem had been solved forever —after the reader had put down the book?

How many matters of absorbing interest must then have been revealed! By means most dexterously disingenuous, Holmes managed a glimpse of

Godfrey Staunton's telegram; and on the first attempt. Yet he had seven different schemes, he told the doctor, if one had failed. What were the other six?

How many, many questions must also have gone unanswered. Holmes was at times blood brother to the Sphinx. There is a bit of dialogue that is in nearly all the tales. "You have a clue?" asks Watson eagerly. The answer is immortal: "It is a capital mistake, my dear Watson, to theorize before one has the facts." If one were called upon to find in literature the best inscription for a tombstone, it would be Holmes's cautious apophthegm. Watson should bargain for it on his grave. For Holmes's tombstone—"Elementary!"

But there can be no grave for Sherlock Holmes or Watson. . . . Shall they not always live in Baker Street? Are they not there this instant, as one writes? . . . Outside, the hansoms rattle through the rain, and Moriarty plans his latest devilry. Within, the sea-coal flames upon the hearth, and Holmes and Watson take their well-won ease. . . . So they still live for all that love them well: in a romantic chamber of the heart: in a nostalgic country of the mind: where it is always 1895.

The Untold Tales of Dr. Watson

"SOMEWHERE in the vaults of the bank of Cox & Company, at Charing Cross," wrote Dr. Watson, in *Thor Bridge,* "there is a travel-worn and battered tin dispatch-box with my name . . . upon the lid. It is crammed with papers, nearly all of which are records of cases to illustrate the curious problems which Mr. Sherlock Holmes had at various times to examine."

Here is treasure trove, indeed!

For years the cry of the hungry populace has been for more tales of Sherlock Holmes—tales which Watson, who presumably still lives amongst us, has for reasons of his own withheld. We have listened to his explanations, at one time and another, and rather fatuously accepted them; but, really, do they explain? With Watson, we may deplore the circumstance that persons of high prominence go right on living, apparently to deprive us of the revelations that would be possible only after their demise; but surely the reputed modesty of Mr. Sherlock Holmes has functioned too often and too conveniently for the good doctor.

The truth may be that Watson's ethical considerations mask a certain indolence and disinclination for which poor Holmes has been made to take the blame. There is little enough, one ventures, in the long record of their association, to corroborate the doctor's assertions that Holmes was so inflexibly opposed to personal publicity. At the moment of triumph, to be sure, the detective invariably waived his right to acclaim, in favour of his friends of Scotland Yard; but after the fact he was usually more than gracious to his biographer. Often he suggested the theme for one of Watson's contributions to the literature of crime; and at no time, one thinks, save where the thing was morally impossible, can his objections have been more than a decent deprecation of his prowess.

On the other hand, the truth may be—in part, at any rate—that Holmes's acid humour was responsible for many of the tantalizing references to cases still unrecorded by his Boswell. His intentional mystification of that humble collaborator is frequently manifest in Watson's pages: what more likely than that the detective, in quizzical temper, whispered hints of extraordinary problems that actually had never come before him? That delicate service which he performed for the reigning family of Holland, perhaps? And the fascinating chapter suggested by the reference to Ricoletti of the Club Foot and his abominable wife?

Poor old Watson! He was easy enough to fool, heaven knows. Did he suspect this to be the case?

If so, somewhat of his embarrassment may be understood. And somewhat of his reticence. Well may he have thought that it were better—far, far better —to stick to problems with the beginning and the end of which he was himself familiar.

Yet, even so, the battered tin dispatch-box must contain—crammed as it is with papers—sufficient of these latter. They will be the notes and records, for the most part, of cases in which Watson played his part. How many of those proverbial little fingers would be sacrificed for just one more small volume of them! Granted that the Baker Street files belonged to Holmes, and have no doubt retired with him to Sussex, beyond the easy reach of Watson's research, it is difficult to see how the doctor can get away from that reckless and revealing reference to his dispatch-box. High time it is, surely, that it were haled forth and compelled to yield its secrets.

*   *   *

On the whole, then, it seems likely enough that Watson's silences, in spite of all his protestations, are to be charged to simple indolence or dereliction. He has been negligent enough, in all conscience, as we have seen before. For one thing, he has told us far too little, really, about himself—a curious omission. Probable as it is that his view of John H. Watson as a mere necessary "property" on the Holmesian stage, was entirely sincere, he could yet be discursively frank, at times—the trusty old creature—about the processes of his not particularly lucid mind. What we lack is a clear record of his life. We know that once he kept a bull pup (it disappeared from the narrative with such celerity that one wonders what became of it), smoked ship's tobacco, enjoyed Beaune with his luncheon, disliked getting up in the morning, used to play Rugby for Blackheath, studied medicine at Bart's, became a military surgeon in the British army, and was wounded at Maiwand during the second Afghan war. We know—thanks to Sherlock Holmes and his deductions from a fifty-guinea watch—that he had an elder brother who drank himself to death. It may seem that we know all that there is to know about John H. Watson—all that it is necessary to know—yet there is much that one would gladly ask him. Not least, perhaps, the truth about the recent crop of rumours that, for a second time—some time presumably in 1902—he took a wife.

There is much, too, that one might ask about the rooms in Baker Street—that theatre upon whose stage so many dramas were enacted with the world for audience; that port from which so many curious craft put forth in London fog or tempest. Little inconsistencies exist which possibly should be explained. One does not hold, however, with those who blame the doctor harshly for his apparent slips of tongue and pen. That Watson's memory was faulty is more than certain; yet it may be that matters now important to his readers seemed un-

important to himself what time he told the tales.
He has been upbraided, for example, because he
has seemed to be inconsistent in his several descrip-
tions of the rooms in Baker Street, with reference
to their exact location in the house. After convey-
ing the impression that all three were on the second
floor, as it would be called in the United States—
seventeen steps, it will be recalled, led upward to
the chambers—he speaks from time to time of going
down to breakfast. It is obvious, however, to the
unprejudiced mind, that a lower room had been
added to the ménage, some time after the original
engagement, and that Watson simply did not think
to mention it. To him it would be relatively unimportant, and no part of his narrative of adventure. In this connection, it should be pointed out
that his precise assertion that the famous sitting-
room was on the *first* floor, is still correct, since in
England the first floor is the first above the level
of the street. The whole house, of course, was
owned or rented by Mrs. Hudson, who was glad
enough, no doubt, to arrange the larger accommo-
dation.

The good doctor's reference to their "bow window" is less easily explained, since—to-day, at any
rate—in all of Baker Street there is no bow window
to be seen. One is of opinion that the careless fellow,
writing loosely and in haste, conceived that any
central aperture was properly so designated.

Of all these little matters, and many others, one

certainly would ask, if opportunity presented. But principally, one would ask about the tales untold —about that box at Charing Cross, crammed with the records of an immortal collaboration. Fragments of mystery, they exist complete in memory —or in anticipation—like tales read long ago and years forgotten; their outlines blur and waver just beyond the edge of thought. It is part of Watson's magic that some of these lost adventures, never set down in print, seem to inhabit the chambers of the mind as memorably as those sixty others that make up the saga.

What was the service for which Holmes refused a knighthood? What were the singular contents of the ancient British barrow? The Conk-Singleton forgery case was certainly in Watson's time and of his knowledge, whatever he may have known—or thought—about the problem that agitated the royal family of Scandinavia. . . . There they lie, the materials for a hundred further stories, in the vaults of Cox & Company, at Charing Cross.

*　　*　　*

Hereafter, for the curious, is set forth in loose order the presumptive titles of certain of the many tales that Watson did not tell. The muster is incomplete; it is a contribution merely to the long list that fancy and deduction might contrive.[1]

[1] The most complete list is to be found in Mr. H. W. Bell's *Sherlock Holmes and Dr. Watson.*

The Case of Mrs. Cecil Forrester.

The Bishopsgate Jewel Case (Inspector Athelney Jones will never forget how Holmes lectured the force upon it!).

The Trepoff Murder Case.

The Singular Tragedy of the Atkinson Brothers at Trincomalee.

The Dundas Separation Case.

The Adventure of the Paradol Chamber.

The Adventure of the Amateur Mendicant Society (whose members held a luxurious club in the lower vault of a furniture warehouse).

The Loss of the British Bark "Sophy Anderson."

The Singular Adventures of the Grice Patersons in the Island of Uffa.

The Camberwell Poisoning Case.

The Tankerville Club Scandal.

The Case of Mrs. Farintosh (which had to do with an opal tiara).

Colonel Warburton's Madness.

The Little Problem of the Grosvenor Square Furniture Van.

The Tarleton Murders.

The Case of Vamberry, the Wine Merchant.

The Adventure of the Old Russian Woman.

The Singular Affair of the Aluminium Crutch.

The Adventure of Ricoletti of the Club Foot and His Abominable Wife (most marvellous of all the missing titles).

The Question of the Netherland-Sumatra Company.

The Colossal Schemes of Baron Maupertuis.

The Manor House Case.

The Adventure of the Tired Captain (Had Mr. E. C. Bentley this case in mind when he wrote *The Inoffensive Captain?*).

The Atrocious Conduct of Colonel Upwood (in connection with the famous card scandal at the Nonpareil Club).

The Case of Mme. Montpensier.

The Papers of Ex-President Murillo.

The Shocking Affair of the Dutch Steamship "Friesland."

The Peculiar Persecution of John Vincent Harden.

The Sudden Death of Cardinal Tosca (an investigation carried out at the personal request of His Holiness, the Pope).

The Case of Wilson, the Notorious Canary Trainer.

The Dreadful Business of the Abernetty Family.

The Conk-Singleton Forgery Case.

The Repulsive Story of the Red Leech.

The Terrible Death of Crosby, the Banker.

The Addleton Tragedy (and the singular contents of the ancient British barrow).

The Smith-Mortimer Succession Case.

The Adventure of the Boulevard Assassin.

The Case of Mr. Fairdale Hobbs.

The Dramatic Adventure of Dr. Moore Agar.

The Giant Rat of Sumatra (a tale revealed in radio drama by Miss Edith Meiser, heaven bless her!).

The Case of Vanderbilt and the Yeggman.

The Hamerford Will Case.

The Case of Vigor, the Hammersmith Wonder.

The Arnsworth Castle Affair.

The Darlington Substitution Scandal.

The Case of Vittoria, the Circus Belle.

The St. Pancras Case.

The Delicate Affair of the Reigning Family of Holland.

The Case of Victor Lynch, the Forger.

The Incredible Mystery of Mr. James Phillimore

(who, stepping back into his own house to get his umbrella, was never more seen in this world).

The Case of the Royal Family of Scandinavia.

The Remarkable Affair of the Cutter "Alicia" (which sailed one spring morning into a small patch of mist from which it never again emerged).

The Intricate Matter in Marseilles.

The Affair of the Politician, the Lighthouse, and the Trained Cormorant.

The Strange Case of Isadora Persano (who was found stark staring mad with a match-box in front of him which contained a remarkable worm said to be unknown to science).

Students are requested to remember, also, that Watson frequently hinted at cases in which his friend was involved, without troubling to give us clues. The important service for which Holmes refused a knighthood—in 1902—is one of these, as is that matter of supreme importance arranged by the great detective for the government of France, during the winter of the year 1890 and the early Spring of 1891.

It is fairly certain, too, that Shinwell Johnson figured as Holmes's underworld deputy in several cases other than that known to us as *The Illustrious Client*. During the early years of the century he was the detective's invaluable assistant in a number of curious matters.

Ave Sherlock Morituri et Cetera

THAT is to say: Hail, Sherlock, we who shall one day pass and be forgotten, salute you, undying, who some say never lived!

Nevertheless, the day will come, one fancies, when Sherlock Holmes will be assumed to have left this mortal life behind. It will be a presumption based on probability, since man—we have been told—may not live forever in the flesh. And when that day shall have arrived, and the sad word have been spoken, there will be records and biographies in number, do not doubt, to prove the facts of his existence. In time, no doubt at all, he will have lived as surely in our world as ever he appeared to live in that span that might have marked his living. There will be little placards on the doors that once he entered, and tall memorials in the pantheons of Christendom. There will be— But already, for the elect, there is that page of reminiscence by Opal, Lady Porstock:

"I need only mention one other of my public activities, which remains a legitimate boast," she asserts, writing of her days in parliament. "It was a Private Member's Bill, brought forward by myself, that procured the erection of the great statue of Sherlock Holmes in Baker Street. I pointed out that London was now the only European capital which had no statue of the kind, and the plaque on No. 221-B Baker Street was a quite inadequate recognition of the famous detective's services. The question whether he ever existed did not affect, or ought not to affect, the feelings of veneration with which we regarded him. When the bill passed, I was elected a member of the Committee which was to decide between the various designs sent in. . . . I am glad to say that it was at my instigation the Committee chose the design sent in by Wrightman, then quite unknown, but destined to become famous as one of the leaders of the neo-classical school of the sixties. The conception is a noble one, and if some have found fault with the pipe as out of keeping with the classical draperies in which the figure is represented, it is not for us to complain." [1]

It is, to be sure, a little early as yet for admirers of Mr. Sherlock Holmes to look up the statue. Lady Porstock would appear to have been writing in the year 1988 of events that transpired between the years 1953 and 1959; and as her valuable reminiscences were edited by Father Ronald Knox in the year 1923, it is fairly obvious that somebody is being spoofed. But one looks forward to the birth of Wrightman, and the coming of the great Baker Street memorial. Already there is a railway engine

[1] R. A. Knox: *Memoirs of the Future.*

wearing the famous name. It runs in and out of the Baker Street Station, and is a sufficiently admirable memorial of its kind.

As Lady Porstock has suggested, the question whether Sherlock ever existed has really nothing to do with the case. Existence is a word that has no very precise definition. It means whatever the prevailing fashion in philosophy wishes it to mean. If it means anything at all, it would appear to mean that which is perceived of the imagination quite as much as that which is real to the primary senses. Certainly it is a commonplace that many things exist which nobody has seen, heard, smelled, tasted, or touched.

* * *

The existence of Sherlock Holmes is, however, something more than a matter of mere faith. That he emerged from the pages of a book may be a concern of scholarly regard, but it can hardly be denied that he has taken his place in the living world. You may go out into the street, if you are in any doubt about it—as Mr. Edward Shanks has suggested—and ask the first bus conductor that you meet. By his own methods, indeed, it could be demonstrated that he lived—nay, that he still lives; and one likes to imagine that, for auld lang syne, he still occasionally revisits the glimpses, in old Baker Street. It was the famous General Humbert, no less, who demanded tidings of the detective, only fifteen years ago. His dinner guest at the moment happened to be Sir Arthur Conan Doyle, then visiting the Argonne.

"*A propos,*" suddenly snapped the General, his hard eyes fixed upon the author's face, "*Sherlock Holmes, est-ce qu'il est un soldat dans l'armée anglaise?*"

There was an embarrassed moment as Sir Arthur paused. Then, "*Mais, mon general,*" stammered the English novelist, "*il est trop vieux pour service.*"

How much too old, Sir Arthur did not say; but Mr. Arthur Bartlett Maurice, excited by the anecdote, determined to find out. On the strength of his researches—and perhaps deductions—he places the detective's birthday in the early fifties; in which event Holmes must to-day be close upon his eightieth anniversary.

Is his mail still heavy, one wonders, there upon the Downs? Innumerable letters have been addressed to him, at one time and another; and by some admirable citizens, too. For the most part, these were sent in care of Sir Arthur Conan Doyle, in the belief that he would forward them; but even when they were not so directed the post-office department of England—an intelligent institution—had no difficulty in making the proper delivery. A number of letters were received by Sir Arthur after it had been announced that Holmes was retiring to his bee farm in Sussex. There were several worthy persons in the world, it appeared, who would be happy to assist him in his project. "Will Mr. Sherlock Holmes require a housekeeper for his country cottage at Xmas?" asked an "old-fashioned, quiet woman" hopefully; and another spread her qualifications on the record: she was an adept, it seemed, at keeping bees and could "segregate the queen."

A professional lecturer who was also an apiarian specialist addressed himself to Sherlock Holmes direct, offering his services in a letter that is singularly charming in its spontaneity and gratitude:

"Dear Sir:—I see by some of the morning papers that you are about to retire and take up bee-keeping. I know not if this be correct or otherwise, but if correct I shall be pleased to render you service by giving any advice you may require. I make this offer in return for the pleasure your writings gave me as a youngster; they enabled me to spend many and many a happy hour. Therefore I trust you will read this letter in the same spirit that it is written."

Autograph-hunters too were pestilential throughout the detective's long career, and doubtless are still bothersome. The more cunning of the tribe, hesitating to approach the celebrity directly, used to address their unctuous requests to Watson, urging his intercession. But the good doctor's most upsetting communication must have been that dictated by a well-known press-cutting agency, suggesting that his brilliant confrère might care to take advantage of its service. That letter, at least, it may be guessed, remained unanswered. There were already, at the time, too many scraps and scrapbooks littering the place to suit the taste of Watson.

But most devout perhaps of all devout believers were those natives of Samoa whose incredible luck it was to have for master a certain Robert Louis Stevenson. Stevenson, telling his own inventions to his servants, in the fragrant Pacific dusk, varied the evening programme with some tales of Sherlock Holmes. In a comical letter to Sir Arthur (not then a knight, however), he complained of the difficulty of telling stories which every moment required a halt for explanations. What, asked the literal Samoans, was a railway? What was an engineer? Somehow, in spite of difficulties, he got the tales across. "If you could have seen the bright feverish eyes of Simite," wrote the Scottish novelist, "you would have tasted glory."

To his own *Bottle Imp* they had listened with bated breath, only to burst forth, at conclusion, with an awkward question: "Where," they demanded eagerly, "is the bottle?"

O ye of little faith! Surely he lived—our Sherlock —and breathed the fog and dust of Baker Street, even as now, one hopes, he breathes the purer air that blows across the Sussex Downs. And Watson too—has he not sold his latest practice, and gone to join his comrade? How often one likes to think that it is so!

*   *   *

But there is still considerable research to be done before those records for the future may be called complete—before the High History of Mr. Sherlock Holmes shall have been set down for posterity. When and where, precisely, was he born? What was the college which for two years he attended? Who and what were his extraordinary parents?—for that they were extraordinary is as certain as that they were unknown to public fame. His brother Mycroft, that colossal genius, that all but fabulous monster, we have casually met on more than one occasion, in the pages of Watson; but about the other members of his family circle Sherlock has been as close-lipped as the dourest Scottish tradesman. Even to Watson he revealed so little of his early life that the doctor was at one time upon the point of believing him an orphan, with no kinsfolk in the world. But with the first mention of his brother Mycroft a few stray facts emerged.

"My ancestors," said Sherlock Holmes, on this unusual occasion, "were country squires, who appear to have led much the same life as is natural to their class. But, none the less, my turn that way [*i. e.*, his ability to observe and make deductions] is in my veins, and may have come with my grandmother, who was the sister of Vernet, the French artist. Art in the blood is liable to take the strangest forms."

His grandmother—but on which side? The mother's, one suspects, since in general his ancestors were English country squires; and is there not perhaps a further clue to family history in Mycroft's name? One offers the suggestion in humility, and yet it may have merit. Mycroft, the elder of two brothers (had there been others, Sherlock, at this time, should have mentioned them), might well receive his mother's family name—a common practice. Possibly even Sherlock was the mother's surname, but indications here point rather to a certain bowler of that name, admired no doubt by Sherlock's unknown father. Young Dr. Verner might resolve the tangle—if he still lives; and if he does, one fears he is no longer young. He it was, it will be remembered, who purchased Watson's practice, in 1894, after the return of Holmes from Switzerland. He paid, it seemed to Watson, a ridiculously high price for so demure a practice; and it was not till some years afterward that Watson found out the truth—that Verner was, in fact, a distant relative of Holmes, and Holmes it was who had turned up the money. The connection here between the younger doctor and that grandmother who was the sister of Vernet is obvious. Verner would be the English form of Vernet, or a corruption of the French name after a year or so in England. And Dr. Verner would be a cousin of the detective, twice or thrice removed.

However that may be, Holmes for two years, we know, attended college, where the only friend he made was Victor Trevor—young Trevor whose father was a J. P. at Donnithorpe, in Norfolk. Old Trevor is, of course, quite dead; but it may be that Victor still survives, in which case there is another source of inquiry. He was last heard of in the Terai, a successful tea-planter. The early friendship came about in curious fashion, when Holmes —upon his way to chapel—was seized by Trevor's bull-terrier and laid up for ten days. It was this acquaintance, it will be remembered, which gave the youthful Sherlock his first case, that celebrated in the *Memoirs* as *The Gloria Scott,* and which really turned his attention to the possibilities of the profession he was so long to grace.

Again, in *The Musgrave Ritual,* there is just a glimpse of Holmes's younger days. He speaks here, easily enough, of his "last years at the university," but presumably it is just a figure of speech. The earlier record seems quite explicit, and it limits Holmes's formal college training to a scant two years. There is also considerable mention of one Reginald Musgrave, with whom at school Holmes had had some acquaintance. Apparently it was nothing intimate, for Musgrave was "not generally popular." Nevertheless, in Musgrave, if he still survives—at Hurlstone Manor, which is in Western Sussex—there is another clue to Holmes's early exploits. Certain it is that his methods had occasioned talk even at the university. It was, indeed, through the good offices, as we know, of former classmates, that several early cases came to him, after he had established himself in London.

His first lodgings were apparently those in Montague Street (mentioned in *The Musgrave Ritual*), just around the corner from the British Museum. "There I waited," Watson tells us the detective told him, "filling in my too abundant leisure time by studying all those branches of science which might make me more efficient." There it was his early clients came to him, among them Reginald Musgrave, whose puzzling problem was chronologically third upon the list. Of the two earlier cases we have no word at all, unless we think of the Trevor business as one of them, which seems unlikely, as it occurred before young Sherlock came to London.

Shortly thereafter, at any rate, it would appear that business picked up, and Sherlock Holmes cast round for larger quarters. He had been for some time, we must suppose, pursuing his curious studies in the chemical laboratory at St. Bartholomew's, where he had become known to young Stamford. All unwitting, and young as he still was, he was now at the turning-point of his career. Almost around the corner—certainly no farther away than the Criterion bar—was Watson. And it can scarcely be denied that it was with Watson's wondering advent that the real career of Sherlock Holmes began.

Thereafter, the materials for a biography are rather numerous. It is of Holmes's younger days that we have need of further information. Is there no anecdote of the precocious youth's first startling piece of observation? His first recorded literary venture set forth by Watson, is a magazine article called *The Book of Life*; but it is certain that his famous monograph *Upon the Distinction Between the Ashes of the Various Tobaccos* was already written—probably also some of his other and less celebrated papers. Those long hours in the rooms in Montague Street would have been admirable for literary enterprise, and it seems highly likely that many of them were thus employed.

* * *

Some day, no doubt, there will be a *Collected Edition* of the famous writings. In the meantime, a bibliography may prove useful, and this immediately follows. The order in which the several items are here set down is not of necessity the order in which they made their original appearance, although an effort has been made to make the muster chronological. Thus:

THE WRITINGS OF MR. SHERLOCK HOLMES

Upon the Distinction Between the Ashes of the Various Tobaccos. "In it," says Holmes, "I enumerate one hundred and forty forms of cigar, cigarette, and pipe tobacco, with coloured plates illustrating the difference in the ash." (*Study in Scarlet, Sign of Four, Boscombe Valley Mystery.*)

Upon the Tracing of Footsteps. "With some remarks

upon the uses of plaster of Paris as a preserver of impresses." (*Sign of Four.*)

Upon the Influence of a Trade upon the Form of the Hand. "With lithotypes of the hands of slaters, sailors, cork-cutters, compositors, weavers, and diamond-polishers." (*Sign of Four.*)

The Book of Life. This was a magazine article on the science of deduction and analysis, based on the author's theories of systematic observation. It probably appeared some time early in 1881. (*Study in Scarlet.*)

On the Typewriter and its Relation to Crime. As early as the late eighties Holmes contemplated the writing of this monograph, and there is no reason to suppose that it was not ultimately accomplished. (*Case of Identity.*)

Upon the Dating of Old Documents. "The *terminus a quo* of this monograph is uncertain," says Mr. S. C. Roberts. "It probably dealt in the main with the problem of handwritings from the sixteenth century onwards. It was completed before the year 1889, and at a later date Holmes was engaged in the study of the mediaeval aspect of the subject." (*Hound of the Baskervilles* and *Golden Pince-Nez.*)

Of Tattoo Marks. "I have made a small study of tattoo marks," says Holmes, "and have even contributed to the literature of the subject." His paper included an examination of the curious pink pigment used by Chinese artists. (*Red-Headed League.*)

On Secret Writings. "I am fairly familiar with all forms of secret writings," Holmes asserts, "and am myself the author of a trifling monograph upon the subject, in which I analyse one hundred and sixty separate ciphers." (*Dancing Men.*)

On the Surface Anatomy of the Human Ear. There were two short monographs on this subject, in the *Anthropological Journal*, apparently some time in the early eighties. Both papers appeared during the one year, and one may well have been an amplification of the other. (*Cardboard Box*.)

Early English Charters. It is not certain that this work ever was completed. Holmes conducted laborious researches in the subject, however, in the year 1895, which led to such striking results that Watson half promised to make them the subject of one of his own narratives—a promise which has not as yet been fulfilled. (*Three Students*.)

On the Polyphonic Motets of Lassus. Printed for private circulation, possibly some time in 1896; certainly later than 1895. This work is said by experts to be the last word upon the subject. (*Bruce-Partington Plans*.)

Chaldean Roots in the Ancient Cornish Language. Holmes began his study of this subject in the spring of 1897, if Watson is correct, and although the adventure of *The Devil's Foot* occurred to interrupt him, it is certain that he returned to it. There is no record of publication, unhappily, but Holmes's interest in the subject would argue that it did ultimately, in some form, achieve the permanence of print. (*Devil's Foot*.)

Malingering. A monograph upon a subject which interested Holmes at the time of the adventure of *The Dying Detective*. While it is not certain that it ever was written, it may very well have been; at least, one fancies, it has become a chapter in his comprehensive textbook, *The Whole Art of Detection*, hereinafter listed. (*Dying Detective*.)

Upon the Uses of Dogs in the Work of the Detective.

It was in 1903 that Holmes first mentioned his intention to write this monograph, but there is no report in Watson of its publication. Possibly it, too, has become merely a chapter in the great textbook of detection. On the other hand, diligent research may turn up a copy of the work as originally planned. (*Creeping Man.*)

Practical Handbook of Bee Culture, with some Observations upon the Segregation of the Queen. This *magnum opus* of the detective's later years was written after his retirement, and was published some time prior to August, 1912. Presumably it is a small 12mo. It was issued in blue cloth, lettered in gold. (*His Last Bow.*)

The Blanched Soldier. The first of the famous detective's criminal reminiscences to be set forth by himself. The adventure occurred in January, 1903, but this account of it was written many years later. It was first published in the *Strand Magazine* during 1926. Available in all editions of *The Case-Book of Sherlock Holmes.* (*Blanched Soldier.*)

The Lion's Mane. Second and last of Holmes's adventures related by himself. The episode is dated in July of 1907, but the reminiscence was probably penned at about the same time as that of *The Blanched Soldier.* Published in the *Strand Magazine* during 1926. Available in all editions of *The Case-Book of Sherlock Holmes.* (*Lion's Mane.*)

Sigerson. It was during the year 1893 that the English newspapers carried accounts of the "remarkable explorations of a Norwegian named Sigerson," who had travelled for two years in Tibet and spent some days with the head Lama, at Lhassa. Sigerson is now known to have been Holmes himself, then believed to be dead; and while the newspaper reports are no doubt interviews rather than first-hand accounts, they will be of the highest interest to all Holmes collectors, and are mentioned here to complete the record. *(Empty House.)*

The Whole Art of Detection. Sherlock Holmes proposed to devote his declining years to the composition of this textbook, which was to "focus the whole art of detection into one volume." He mentioned it to Watson on a cold morning in the winter of 1897, and there is no reason to suppose that he ever gave over the fascinating idea. As the volume has not yet been announced, it may be assumed that it is still in preparation. *(Abbey Grange.)*

Translations. The number of Holmes's works that have been translated into foreign languages is probably large, and no attempt has been made to run them all to earth. Certain it is that as early as 1888 François le Villard was engaged in translating the writings then published, into French; and where the French were adventuring it is certain the Germans were not far behind. The two criminal reminiscences (see above) have appeared in practically *all* languages, including the Scandinavian.

Look well, then, for all these rare and difficult titles, bookmen, for your own shelves and for the records of the future. In them are the exercises of a great and vigorous mind unhampered by the interruptions and the cries of Watson. Good fellow, he has spoiled some admirable monologues, at one time and another, by his appalling muddleheadedness.

The Real Sherlock Holmes

But one must drop, at last, the happy pretense; admit that Sherlock Holmes is dead. And being dead yet liveth. The paradox is complete; the tale is ended. The greatest detective of the modern world has gone, at length, upon his final quest, the most mysterious of all his strange adventures.

He died upon the 7th of July, the year being 1930, at his home in Crowborough, Sussex—Windlesham, he called it—in the person of the man who had created him. For true as it may be that the model for the immortal detective was Dr. Joseph Bell of Edinburgh, there can be little doubt that the real Holmes was Conan Doyle himself. In innumerable ways throughout his life of extraordinary service, the British novelist demonstrated the truth of the assertion. From first to last—as student, physician, writer, spiritualist, and prophet of the war—he was always the private detective, the seeker after hidden truths, the fathomer of obscure mysteries, the hound of justice upon the trail of injustice and official apathy.

It was inevitable that the author of the Sherlock Holmes stories should often be called upon to enact the rôle of his imaginary detective, and not infrequently he accepted the implied challenge. Twice in his career he undertook fatiguing causes, because he believed that justice had not been done. The cases of George Edalji and Oscar Slater were notorious in their day. They shook all England, and the thunder of Doyle's denunciations crossed the Atlantic. Twenty years and more have since elapsed, yet echoes of the famous cases still reverberate; and it was only recently that the convict Slater, championed by the indignant novelist, won his freedom from prison—and revealed his singular ingratitude.

There is a flavour of the Holmes tales in both episodes—that pinch of the bizarre, bordering on the fantastic, that marks most of the fictive adventures. Chronologically the Edalji case stands first. The facts are as follows:

George Edalji, a young law student, was the son of a certain Rev. S. Edalji, a Parsee, yet vicar of the Anglican Parish of Great Wyrley, whose wife was an English woman. The vicar was a kindly, intelligent man who performed his churchly duties with fidelity. His wife was an excellent wife. Their son, the half-caste George Edalji, was a young man of irreproachable character, and an admirable student who had won the highest honours in his legal studies. Nevertheless, the situation was unfortunate. "How the vicar came to be a Parsee," wrote

Conan Doyle, "or how the Parsee came to be the vicar, I have no idea. Perhaps some catholic-minded patron wished to demonstrate the universality of the Anglican church. The experiment will not, I hope, be repeated, for though the vicar was an amiable and devoted man, the appearance of a coloured clergyman with a half-caste son in a rude, unrefined parish was bound to cause some regrettable situation." [1]

The family became the target for considerable local malice, and was for a time subjected to a veritable broadside of anonymous letters, many of them "of the most monstrous description." Shortly thereafter an epidemic of horse-maiming broke out, and these outrages lasted for a considerable period. The police accomplished next to nothing until popular clamour forced an activity; then a hurried investigation was conducted and George Edalji was arrested for the crime—that is, for the crime of horse-maiming. The principal evidence against him was found in certain of the anonymous letters, in which the writer hinted at a knowledge of the crimes involving horses. It was asserted that George Edalji had written the letters which for so long had plagued his family.

This evidence, as later pointed out by Doyle, was incredibly weak; yet the police, "all pulling together and twisting all things to their end," secured

---

[1] A. C. Doyle: *Memories and Adventures.*

a conviction, and the prisoner was sentenced to seven years' penal servitude. This was in 1903.

* * *

It was not until late in 1906 that Sir Arthur heard of the rather obscure case; then a statement of it caught his eye in an unimportant journal. "As I read," he later wrote, "the unmistakable accent of truth forced itself upon my attention and I realized that I was in the presence of an appalling tragedy, and that I was called upon to do what I could to set it right." This included a careful reading of everything he could obtain bearing upon the case, a study of the trial, a visit to the family of the condemned man, and a tour of investigation over the scene of the several crimes. Early in 1907 he began publication of a series of articles analyzing the evidence,[1] and shortly England and the English-speaking world was ringing with the wrongs of George Edalji.

"If the whole land had been raked, I do not think it would have been possible to find a man who was so unlikely, and indeed so incapable of committing such actions," wrote Sir Arthur, in his autobiography. "Nothing in his life had ever been urged against him. His old schoolmaster with years of experience testified to his mild and tractable disposition. He had served his time with a Birmingham solicitor, who gave him the highest references.

[1] A. C. Doyle: *The Case of Mr. George Edalji.*

He had never shown traits of cruelty. He was . . . devoted to his work . . . and he had already at the age of twenty-seven written a book upon Railway Law. Finally, he was a total abstainer, and so blind that he was unable to recognize anyone at the distance of six yards. It was clear that the inherent improbability of such a man committing a long succession of bloody and brutal crimes was so great that it could only be met by the suggestion of insanity. There had never, however, been any indication even of eccentricity in George Edalji. On the contrary, his statements of defense were measured and rational, and he had come through a series of experiences which might well have unhinged a weaker intellect."

One hears the familiar voice of Sherlock Holmes himself in such a statement.

It had been charged at the trial that Edalji had committed the mutilations for which he was being tried, at some time in the evening. The prisoner was able to prove a certain alibi, however, so the police dexterously shifted ground and advanced a new theory—to wit, that the crimes had been committed in the early hours of the morning. As against this, it was shown that George Edalji slept in the same room as his father, the Parsee vicar, who was not only a light sleeper but in the habit of locking the door of the chamber each night before he retired. The vicar swore that his son had never left the room during the night.

"This may not constitute an absolute alibi in the eye of the law," comments Sir Arthur dryly, "but it is difficult to imagine anything nearer to one unless a sentinel had been placed outside the door all night."

But the defence of Edalji was weakly conducted. As far as Conan Doyle was able to discover, no mention ever was made of the fact that the prisoner was virtually blind—save in a good light—while between his home and the scene of the mutilations stretched the breadth of the London and North-Western Railway, a complex expanse of rails and wires and other obstacles, with hedges upon either side, difficult enough for any man to pass in daylight.

All of which, and much more, was set forth by Sir Arthur in his indignant articles; and so great was the storm he stirred up that a government committee was appointed to examine and report. The finding, when at length it came to hand, was a compromise. The committee was severe enough upon the condemnation of Edalji and could find no evidence to associate him with the crime, but it clung stubbornly to the old theory that he had written the anonymous letters—which were in two handwritings—and had been, therefore, himself contributory to the miscarriage of justice. Edalji was freed but was denied compensation for his long incarceration. "A blot upon the record of English justice," Sir Arthur called it, in his later writings;

and he added: "It is to be remembered that the man was never tried for writing the letters—a charge which could not have been sustained—so that as the matter stands he has got no redress for three years of false imprisonment, on the score that he did something else for which he has never been tried."

*　　*　　*

But Sir Arthur in his Sherlockian explorations at Wyrley had found what seemed to him a direct clue to the writer or writers of the letters, and also to the identity of the mutilator or mutilators. "I became interested," he tells us in *Memories and Adventures,* "the more so as the facts were very complex and I had to do with people who were insane as well as criminal. I have several letters threatening my life in the same writing as those which assailed the Edaljis—a fact which did not appear to shake in the least the Home Office conviction that George Edalji had written them all. . . . The mistake I made was that having got on the track of the miscreant, I let the police and the Home Office know my results before they were absolutely completed. There was a strong prima facie case, but it needed the good will and co-operation of the authorities to ram it home. That co-operation was wanting . . . The law officers of the Crown upheld their view that there was not a prima facie case . . . Let me briefly state the case that the public may judge. I will call the suspect 'X'. I was able to show:

"1. That 'X' had shown a peculiar knife or horse-lancet to someone and had stated that this knife did the crimes. I had this knife in my possession.

"2. That this knife or a similar knife must have been used in *some* of the crimes, as shown by the shallow incision.

"3. That 'X' had been trained in the slaughter-yard and the cattleship, and was accustomed to brutal treatment of animals.

"4. That he had a clear record both of anonymous letters and of destructive propensities.

"5. That his writing and that of his brother exactly fitted into the two writings of the anonymous letters. In this I had strong independent evidence.

"6. That he had shown signs of periodical insanity, and that his household and bedroom were such that he could leave unseen at any hour of the night.

"There were very many corroborative evidences, but those were the main ones, coupled with the fact that when 'X' was away for some years the letters and outrages stopped, but began again when he returned. On the other hand, when Edalji was put in prison the outrages went on the same as before."

A very workmanlike summary, one thinks, and quite worthy of Sherlock Holmes at his best. It may be added that Sir Arthur later learned that the individual referred to as "X" had been convicted a number of times and for a number of crimes including arson, theft, and damage. Nothing ever was done for Edalji, however, after his release—except by individuals. "He came to my wedding reception," Doyle has recorded, "and there was no guest whom I was prouder to see."

* * *

The Slater case, the celebrity of which was greater than that of George Edalji, came to the detective-novelist as a result of the earlier investigation. It was believed by Slater sympathizers that what Sir Arthur could do for one man he could do for another. "I went into the matter most reluctantly," his autobiography asserts, "but when I glanced at the facts, I saw that it was an even worse case than the Edalji one, and that this unhappy man had in all probability no more to do with the murder for which he had been condemned than I had. I am convinced that when on being convicted he cried out to the judge that he never knew that such a woman as the murdered woman existed he was speaking the literal truth."

The victim was a Miss Marion Gilchrist, an elderly spinster living in Glasgow. She was murdered in her flat, in which she had lived for thirty years, on the 21st of December, 1908. Her servant, Helen Lambie, was out of the place at the time, purchasing a newspaper, and it was during her ten-minute absence that the murder was committed. Returning from her errand, the servant found a young man named Adams at the Gilchrist door, ringing the bell. He was from the flat below. He and his sisters had heard a noise above, in Miss Gilchrist's apartment, and a heavy fall, and he had been sent upstairs to ascertain what had happened. The servant opened the door with her key. Then as they hesitated on the threshold, a man appeared from within, who approached them pleasantly, seemed about to speak, but instead passed them and rushed down the stairs. In the dining room the body of Miss Gilchrist was found, the head brutally beaten in and covered with a rug.

In spite of the fact that Miss Gilchrist was the possessor of a valuable collection of jewelry, robbery would appear not to have been the motive for the murder, since all that was missing was a crescent diamond brooch worth possibly fifty pounds. A box of papers had been broken open and the contents scattered. The description of the man seen by Adams and Helen Lambie was not particularly good, as reported by them; they were in some disagreement: and it was not at all the description of Oscar Slater, a German Jew by extraction, who was ultimately arrested and condemned for the crime.

The apprehension of Slater came about because he had pawned a diamond brooch just before starting for America. New York was warned of his expected advent on American shores and he was arrested and returned to Glasgow, where it was discovered beyond a question of doubt that the brooch in question had been in his possession for years and never had belonged to Miss Gilchrist.

The public had lost its head, however, and the police were in similar state. Slater was poor and without friends. His morals were shown not to have been of the highest, and Scottish virtue was shocked. A card of tools was found in his belongings, and it was seriously asserted that the small hammer of the set had been the instrument of death. The description of the man seen by Adams and Lambie was amended to fit Slater. The two principal witnesses were not sure, but thought the man they had seen in the hallway might have been the prisoner. The frameup may not have been deliberate, but it was a frameup. Slater was in bad case. He proved a clear alibi, but as his witnesses were his mistress and his servant girl it was not allowed. No attempt ever was made to show a connection between Slater and Miss Gilchrist, or between Slater and anybody in the house occupied by Miss Gilchrist. He was a stranger in Glasgow. At the trial he was not too well defended, and the Crown ultimately won a conviction—under Scottish law—by a vote of nine ballots to six. Slater was condemned to death, the scaffold was erected, and two days before the day set for the execution the sentence was commuted. He was resentenced to life imprisonment and was serving his sentence when Arthur Conan Doyle became interested in his plight.

* * *

In Sir Arthur's brilliant pamphlet, *The Case of Oscar Slater,* now a rarity, there is all the fascination of a tale from the chronicles of Sherlock Holmes. Many of its assertions, dogmatic and otherwise, might indeed have been quoted direct from those old pages. Is not this, for instance, the veritable accent of Holmes, talking to the faithful Watson?

"The trouble, however, with all police prosecutions is that, having once got what they imagine to be their man, they are not very open to any line of investigation which might lead to other conclusions. Everything which will not fit into the official theory is liable to be excluded. One might make a few isolated comments on the case which may at least give rise to some interesting trains of thought."

And, for a beginning, Sir Arthur wonders if the murderer was really after the jewels at all. . . . "When he reached the bedroom and lit the gas, he did not at once seize the watch and rings which were lying openly exposed upon the dressing-table. He did not pick up a half-sovereign which was lying on the dining-room table. His attention was given to a wooden box, the lid of which he wrenched open. The papers in it were strewed on the ground. Were the papers his object, and the final abstraction of one diamond brooch a mere blind?"

But, supposing the murderer to have been indeed after the jewels, "it is very instructive to note his knowledge of their location, and also its limitations. Why did he go straight into the spare bedroom where the jewels were actually kept? The same question may be asked with equal force if we consider that he was after the papers. Why the spare bedroom? Any knowledge gathered from outside (by a watcher in the back-yard, for example) would go to the length of ascertaining which was the old lady's room. One would expect a robber who had gained his information thus, to go straight to that chamber. But this man did not do so. He went straight to the unlikely room in which both jewels and papers actually were. Is not this remarkably suggestive? Does it not pre-suppose a previous acquaintance with the inside of the flat and the ways of its owner?

"But now note the limitations of the knowledge. If it were the jewels he was after, he knew what room they were in, but not in what part of the room. A fuller knowledge would have told him they were kept in the wardrobe. And yet he searched a box. . . . To this we may add that he would seem to have shown ignorance of the habits of the inmates, or he would surely have chosen Lambie's afternoon or evening out for his attempt, and not have done it at a time when the girl was bound to be back within a very few minutes. What men had ever visited the house? The number must have been very limited. What friends? what trades-men? what plumbers?"

Surely that is all good Sherlock Holmes, as—even more brilliantly—is this: "How did the murderer get in if Lambie is correct in thinking that she shut the doors? I cannot get away from the conclusion that he had duplicate keys. In that case all becomes comprehensible, for the old lady—whose faculties were quite normal—would hear the lock go and would not be alarmed, thinking that Lambie had returned before her time. Thus, she would only know her danger when the murderer rushed into the room, and would hardly have time to rise, re-ceive the first blow, and fall, as she was found, be-side the chair upon which she had been sitting. But if he had *not* the keys, consider the difficulties. If the old lady had opened the flat door her body would have been found in the passage. Therefore, the police were driven to the hypothesis that the old lady heard the ring, opened the lower stair door from above (as can be done in all Scotch flats), opened the flat door, never looked over the lighted stair to see who was coming up, but returned to her chair and her magazine, leaving the door open and a free entrance to the murderer. This is pos-sible, but is it not in the highest degree improb-able? Miss Gilchrist was nervous of robbery and would not neglect obvious precautions. The ring came immediately after the maid's departure. She could hardly have thought that it was her (*sic*) returning, the less so as the girl had the keys and would not need to ring."

The only alternatives to this reasoning, ventured Sir Arthur, were that "the murderer was actually concealed in the flat when Lambie came out, and of that there is no evidence whatever, or that the visitor was someone whom the old lady knew, in which case he would naturally have been admitted."

Sir Arthur's narrative points out that although the crime was a singularly bloody one, no marks of blood were found on match or matchbox, and none upon the wooden box opened in the bedroom. "It has never been explained why a rug was laid over the murdered woman. . . . It is at least possible that he (*i. e.*, the murderer) used the rug as a shield between him and his victim while he battered her with his weapon. His clothes, if not his hands, would in this way be preserved."

In a brilliant examination of the evidence produced at the trial, the novelist questions the qualities of the witnesses, stresses the important fact that a knowledge of Miss Gilchrist's jewel collection was not, at the time of the murder, confined to the inmates of the house, and emphasizes the significant circumstance that a dog belonging to Miss Gilchrist had been poisoned in September of the year 1908—that is to say, more than a month before Slater arrived in Glasgow and more than two months before the murder. In his pamphlet he is very severe upon the Scottish Lord-Advocate who conducted the prosecution.

* * *

All in all, it is a masterly document, ringing in every line with the curt inflections of Sherlock Holmes himself, and charged with that detective's hard logic and common sense. However, it was to no immediate purpose. The novelist's newspaper campaign stirred England and even brought about another government commission to inquire into the affair; but nothing came of it, and Slater was allowed to languish in prison.

A strange aftermath of the case is recorded by Sir Arthur in his autobiography. Shortly after the trial of Slater messages were received in a Spiritualist circle, which purported to come from the murdered woman. She was asked what weapon had slain her, and replied that it had been an iron box-opener—a singularly satisfying answer, according to Conan Doyle, considering the peculiar nature of the wounds upon the head. The writer also asserts that the name of the murderer was asked and a reply given, but he does not reveal the name.

There for years the unhappy affair rested. From time to time, as Slater's incarceration lengthened, efforts were made to reopen the case, but in actuality it was nineteen years after the conviction before Sir Arthur's activities were successful. Then, at long last, Slater was released—in July of 1928. According to newspaper reports, he accepted a government offer of £6,000 as compensation for his wrongs; then with strange ingratitude refused to repay a sum of money guaranteed by Doyle before the retrial at which he was acquitted.

"I had to guarantee £1,000," asserted Sir Arthur to a press representative. "After his release I raised £700 by subscription and paid the balance myself. When Slater received £6,000 compensation from the government and large sums from the newspapers, I asked him to refund my £300, but with incredible and monstrous ingratitude he refused. He is not a murderer, but an ungrateful dog, and I think the Scottish nation should repay me."

Slater, smoking a large cigar at a Brighton hotel, after a couple of rounds at golf, merely shrugged. "I can not pay," he said. "All my money is invested in annuities and though I made £2,000 from newspaper articles after my release, Doyle did nearly as well."

*   *   *

Minor mysteries were frequently presented for Sir Arthur's solution, he sets forth in his account of his adventures, and it was his pleasure, when in a detective mood, to put his wits to work upon the problems. In one, the habits of thought made familiar by Mr. Sherlock Holmes of Upper Baker Street were copied with entire success. The case was that of a man who had disappeared after withdrawing his bank balance of £40, for which sum it was feared he had been slain. The last trace of the supposed victim was at a large hotel in London; he had come up from the country only that morning. In the evening he was known to have visited a theatre, then to have returned to his hotel and changed from his evening garments into walking clothes. The evening raiment was found the next day in his room. No one saw him leave the hotel, but a guest in a neighbouring room asserted that he had heard the man moving about during the night. A week had elapsed when the novelist was consulted, and the police had discovered exactly nothing. A perfect opening for an adventure of Sherlock Holmes.

The facts were communicated by relatives of the missing man, living in the country, and Sir Arthur answered by return post that, obviously, the vanished citizen was either in Glasgow or Edinburgh. It was later proved that he had gone to Edinburgh. One can almost hear the cry of the admiring Watson—"Wonderful, my dear Holmes!"—and the retort of the detective—"Elementary, my dear Watson, elementary!"

"The one advantage which I possessed," explains Sir Arthur in *Memories and Adventures,* "was that I was familiar with the routine of London hotels.

The first thing was to look at the facts and separate what was certain from what was conjecture. It was *all* certain except the statement of the person who heard the missing man in the night. How could he tell such a sound from any other sound in a large hotel? That point could be disregarded if it traversed the general conclusions. The first deduction was that the man had meant to disappear. Why else should he draw all his money? He had got out of the hotel during the night. But there is a night porter in all hotels, and it is impossible to get out without his knowledge when the door is once shut. The door is shut after the theatre-goers return— say at twelve o'clock. He had come from the music-hall at ten, had changed his clothes, and had departed with his bag. No one had seen him do so. The inference is that he had done it at the moment when the hall was full of the returning guests, which is from eleven to eleven-thirty. After that hour, even if the doors were still open, there are few people coming and going, so that he with his bag would certainly have been seen.

"Having got so far upon firm ground, we now ask ourselves why a man who desires to hide himself should go out at such an hour. If he intended to conceal himself in London he need never have gone to the hotel at all. Clearly then he was going to catch a train which would carry him away. But a man who is deposited by a train in any provincial station during the night is likely to be noticed, and he might be sure that when the alarm was raised and his description given some guard or porter would remember him. Therefore, his destination would be some large town which he would reach as a terminus where all his fellow passengers would disembark and where he would lose himself in the crowd. When one turns up the time-table and sees that the great Scotch expresses bound for Edinburgh and Glasgow start about midnight, the goal is reached. As for his dress suit, the fact that he abandoned it proved that he intended to adopt a line of life where there were no social amenities. This deduction also proved to be correct."

In another case, involving a young woman engaged to be married to a foreigner, the man also disappeared and by a similar process of reasoning Sir Arthur was able to show where he had gone and how unworthy he was of his fiancée's affection.

Not all the novelist's detective cases, however, were as successful as these. He relates with great gusto how, on the occasion of a burglary within a stone's throw of his own home, the village constable—with no theories at all—had actually seized the culprit when he (Sir Arthur) had got no farther than the Sherlockian conclusion that the man was left-handed and had nails in his shoes.

Even in his spiritualistic investigations, which occupied the later years of his life to the exclusion of almost everything else, the novelist was at all times the detective, applying the methods of his most famous fictive character to the obscure problems of psychic phenomena. Not many years before his death he examined the curious claim of a number of children that they had seen and photographed living fairies; he even published a volume on the subject. To the end he was a remarkable example of the scientific investigator touched with the curiosity and credulity of a child—an admirable blend, it would seem, for the perfect sleuth.

Impersonators of
Mr. Sherlock Holmes

THERE is a line of text in Watson from which we learn that all emotions, and particularly that of love, were abhorrent to the "cold, precise, but admirably balanced mind" of Mr. Sherlock Holmes. Nevertheless, it is of record that Holmes once fell in love and married. Since it was only on the stage, perhaps it does not count. Miss Alice Faulkner was the woman in the case, however, and as recently as 1930 her golden head was still lying upon the detective's shoulder at final curtain fall.

The year was 1899 when this astonishing event began to happen; it shared honours with the Boer War. Sir Arthur Conan Doyle, still three years short of knighthood, at his pleasant home called Undershaw, in Surrey, received a sudden wire from an American actor whom he had given permission to write a play called *Sherlock Holmes*.

"May I marry Holmes?" the swift, brief cable asked.

And Conan Doyle, then worrying about the war and how he might get into it, replied: "You may marry or murder or do what you like with him."

Mr. William Gillette elected to marry him—with consequences that have been at once historic and pleasing to everyone concerned. "I was charmed both with the play, the acting, and the pecuniary result," Sir Arthur testified in later years—the "both" being, no doubt, a piece of literary haste that he forgot to catch in proof. For thirty years, at any rate, the public and the box office have echoed that applause.

An absurd, preposterous, and thoroughly delightful melodrama, Mr. Gillette's *Sherlock Holmes* is possibly, as Frederic Dorr Steele has said of it, the best realization of a novelist's conception ever produced upon the stage. With admirable ingenuity, the actor-playwright blended some six or seven of the famous tales into a perfect whole, inventing when he cared to, and achieved a new adventure that was as fresh and crisp as anything from Watson's notebooks. Principally, the play grew out of three celebrated episodes—*A Scandal in Bohemia, The Final Problem,* and *A Study in Scarlet,* in that curiously inverted order—but there are lines and glimpses of certain other tales so skillfully interpolated and so subtly changed as almost to defy the expert. The work is thus at once an adaptation and a creation; and as a whole the credit is largely Gillette's. Certain it is that neither Doyle nor Watson ever saw the manuscript. The play, however, as they have said, delighted them.

Upon the stage it was a thunderous success.

"Gillette," said Professor James Weber Linn, with fine analysis, on the occasion of the last revival, "was born for melodrama because he believes in melodrama. His convictions, his nervousness, his intensity, highlight everything. . . . Situation is his god, emotion the burnt offering upon its altar, and his technique is a priest-lke control. Touch an icicle with a certain chemical and it will burst into flame. That is the laboratory experiment which Gillette carries out in all his best scenes."

It was to the professor that George Fitch whispered, on an earlier occasion: "We are all Watsons to his Holmes!"

The story needs no retelling. Who that has seen the play (and who has *not* seen it?) will forget the Larrabees—that admirable pair of scoundrels—and the strange case of Miss Alice Faulkner? Recovery of the precious "papers" was too perilous a task, however, even for the Larrabees, with Sherlock Holmes upon the job; and hence—Professor Moriarty. He is called Robert in the play. One thanks the playwright for that information—it was a name apparently unknown to Watson. *Robert Moriarty!* Did Holmes himself, one wonders, know that the professor's name was Robert? The original of Moriarty was Adam Worth, who stole the famous Gainsborough, in 1876, and hid it for a quarter of a century,[1] but even that master criminal might have

---

[1] This was revealed by Sir Arthur in conversation with Dr. Gray Chandler Briggs, some years ago.

taken lessons from the Moriarty of Holmes and Watson, a figure of colossal resource and malevolence.

*   *   *

The play opened at the Garrick Theatre, in New York, on November 6, 1899, and ran there for 230 performances. Subsequently it played a year upon the road; and finally—in 1901—it went to England to play a triumphant season at Sir Henry Irving's *Lyceum*. Since that far time there have been revivals in number, not all of them conducted by Mr. Gillette himself, and the play has been seen in stock. In the detective's part, only Gillette is thinkable, although in its time—and theirs—it has been essayed by the late Herbert Kelcey and a host of others. The original Dr. Watson was the late Bruce McRae, while—charming to recount—an early English "Billy" was no less a person than "Master Charles Chaplin," an orphan boy of talent, destined to write his name across the sky in letters which for lustre challenge those that celebrate the fame of Sherlock Holmes.

Chaplin never played the part in America; but again, in 1905, when Gillette took his *Clarice* to the English capital, "Charlie" was the dapper "Billy" in a curtain-raiser that has been lost, one fears, to literature and the stage. *The Painful Predicament of Sherlock Holmes* it was called, and King Edward VII, who witnessed the performance at the *Duke of York's,* read the names of the performers from a programme of white satin:

Gwendolyn Cobb	Miss Irene Vanbrugh
Sherlock Holmes	Mr. William Gillette
Billy	Master Charles Chaplin

Mr. Hannen Swaffer records the episode; and Mr. Gillette remembers the predicament. It involved a young woman of excessive volubility, who talked such a steady and passionate stream at the detective that he had no chance himself to say a word. With the help of Billy, however, he managed to get her out.

Conceivably the greatest triumph of the play was its last revival by Gillette; one does not say the latest, for it is likely that it was indeed the last. This occurred in 1929 and 1930, and it was a victorious occasion. Complicated by sentiment, and by historical importance, as the situation was, the curious charm of the old play persisted. Oldsters turned out to relive their memories of thirty years and youngsters to discover what it was their parents had been shouting about. Back of it, of course, as always, lay the stupendous legend of Sherlock Holmes—an illusion unique in profane letters. In the midst of it strode the ageing, angular figure of the actor who had done as much to create that illusion as Conan Doyle and John H. Watson themselves.

Conan Doyle lived just long enough to congratulate his stage detective upon the great revival. "May I add a word to those which are addressed to you upon the occasion of your return to the stage?" he wrote. "That this return should be in *Sherlock Holmes* is, of course, a source of personal gratification, my only complaint being that you make the poor hero of the anaemic printed page a very limp object as compared with the glamour of your own personality which you infuse into his stage presentment. . . . But in any case you are bringing back to the world something very precious in your own great powers, and I rejoice to know it."

The gratitude of America was expressed by Booth Tarkington in a memorable sentence: "Your return to the stage is a noble and delightful event, and, speaking for myself, I would rather see you play Sherlock Holmes than be a child again on Christmas morning."

* * *

In the early nineteen-hundreds the first successor to the masterpiece appeared—an opus based upon *The Sign of Four*—and met with considerable success in various cities of the Middle West; nor did it fail to thrill its thousands when produced in Philadelphia and New York. Its author God alone remembers. Highly melodramatic and Grand Guignol in its flavour, it played to crowded popular theatres for a time, then vanished from the world.

WILLIAM GILLETTE AS SHERLOCK HOLMES

It was unknown, apparently, to Conan Doyle, and probably unauthorized; but chronologically it wears the second ribbon. Who played the gaunt detective in this fortuitous divertissement one finds no memory long enough to say.

There was no authorized successor to Gillette till 1910, in which year Conan Doyle himself vouchsafed one. After the withdrawal of his *House of Temperley* from a large London theatre on which he held a six months' lease, Sir Arthur, facing serious loss, determined—he writes—"to play a bold and energetic game." His account of it, as set forth in his *Memories and Adventures,* is diverting reading. . . .

"When I saw the course that things were taking, I shut myself up and devoted my whole mind to making a sensational Sherlock Holmes drama. I wrote it in a week and called it *The Speckled Band,* after a short story of that name. I do not think that I exaggerate if I say that within a fortnight of the one play shutting down I had a company working upon the rehearsals of a second one, which had been written in the interval. It was a considerable success. Lyn Harding, as the half epileptic and wholly formidable Doctor Grimesby Rylott, was most masterful, while [H. A.] Saintsbury as Sherlock Holmes was also very good. Before the end of the run I had cleared off all that I had lost upon the other play, and I had created a permanent property of some value. It became a stock piece and is even now [1924] touring the country.

"We had a fine rock boa to play the title-rôle, a snake which was the pride of my heart, so one can imagine my disgust when I saw that one critic ended his disparaging review by the words, 'The crisis of the play was produced by the appearance of a palpably artificial serpent.' I was inclined to offer him a goodly sum if he would undertake to go to bed with it. We had several snakes at different times, but they were none of them born actors and they were all inclined either to hang down from the hole in the wall like inanimate bell-pulls, or else to turn back through the hole and get even with the stage carpenter who pinched their tails in order to make them more lively. Finally we used artificial snakes, and every one, including the stage carpenter, agreed that it was more satisfactory."

When this melodrama was produced in America Mr. Harding continued in the part of Dr. Grimesby Rylott, and the rôle of Sherlock Holmes was capably performed by Mr. H. Cooper-Cliffe.

* * *

The Hound of the Baskervilles also has been produced upon the stage; but, as in the case of *The Sign of Four*, the production was presumably unheard of by the Hound's creator, and records of the play are not available. It is asserted, how-

ever, by Dr. Gray C. Briggs of St. Louis—a dev-
otee of Sherlock Holmes since he was able to lisp
the word "detective"—to have been done in German, by a capable company, at the Odeon Theatre, in St. Louis, during the winter of 1913—at
which time the eminent Missouri physician and
Sherlockian was a member of one of the audiences.
This German version of the *Hound* was, in all
probability, an importation from the Fatherland,
for it is certain that several dramas based on the
adventures of the great detective have been produced in Germany.

France and Spain, also, as well as Russia, Japan,
and probably other nations, witnessed performances of Sherlock Holmes adventures. In Berlin,
a translation of the Gillette melodrama was received with acclamation, during 1905; and a few
years later the French version was one of the great
successes of the Parisian stage. This French version, for which M. Pierre de Courcelle was responsible, follows closely the lines of the Gillette
production, but differs radically in the final act.
Also, the names of several of the characters are
changed—Larrabee is known as Orlebarre, Sidney
Prince as John Alfred Napoleon Bribb, and Alice
Faulkner as Alice Brent. It is Bribb, not Moriarty,
who is captured by Holmes in the de Courcelle
version, when the darbies are snapped upon the
burly cabman—a jolly deviation from the original

that leaves the scoundrel Moriarty still at large for Holmes and M. de Courcelle to capture in an added act.

It is an ingenious addition—that final act—based on the *Adventure of the Empty House,* with variations. The stage, divided into three parts, after the fashion of a triptych, reveals in the center panel an impression of the street, upon the left the living-room of Sherlock Holmes, and on the right the dark and dingy chamber of the Empty House, across the way. Into the empty room steal Moriarty and one of his associates; in the lighted living-room is revealed the figure of Sherlock Holmes, upon a couch—asleep. There is a whir-ring *click* as the Professor's airgun speaks, and the recumbent figure in the living-room topples to the floor. Then the familiar and dreaded voice of the detective is at the miscreant's ear, as Holmes and his assistants (from the Yard) spring out upon the criminal and bear him to the ground. The figure on the couch was just a waxen dummy.

The success of this captivating absurdity is said to have been annoying to the Parisian police, who, during the remarkable run of more than 300 per-formances, had their hands full discouraging the numerous citizens who imagined themselves to be either Moriartys or incarnations of Sherlock Holmes. M. Gemier, it should be added, was the French actor who impersonated the detective; his interpretation—however Gallicized a variant—is reported to have been a striking one.

* * *

In Spain, the popularity of the detective, upon the stage and otherwise, has been enormous. The Iberian imagination reacted warmly to the famous sleuth, almost from the beginnings of his career. It endowed him with Spanish qualities and a Spanish cast of countenance; it produced an endless number of dime-novel adventures that were quite unknown to Watson; and in the end the stage claimed him in dramas that were, in several instances, the original work of native dramatists—involving him in combat with celebrated criminals of fiction for whom neither Doyle nor Watson ever were responsible. For almost equally popular in Spain have been the romantic figures or Arsène Lupin and Raffles.

The first dramatic work produced in Spain, in which the lean detective figured, according to Professor P. P. Rogers of Oberlin, was a *zarzuela*— *Holmes y Raffles*—by Gonzalo Jóver and Emilio Gonzalez del Castillo. It was followed by a sequel, *La garra de Holmes, segunda parte de Holmes y Raffles*, written by the same authors, who requested that the two works be played together. Both pieces were produced at the *Teatro Martin*, June 15, 1908.

This was the opening gun. Thereafter, Señor

Sherlock appeared with frequency upon the Spanish stage. His favourite foe was the intrepid Raffles —who, in the epidemic literature of Spain, is John C. Raffles. In Hornung's pages that exceptional cricketer was called A. J. Inspired by the apocryphal adventures of both celebrities—flowing daily from certain Barcelona presses in floods of gaudy pamphlets—two other gentlemen of letters collaborated to exploit the famous adversaries. Their five-act thriller, *La captura de Raffles, o el triunfo de Holmes*—by Luis Millá y Gacio and Guillermo X. Roura—was produced at Barcelona in November of 1908, and succeeded in the following year by its inevitable sequel, *Nadie más fuerte que Sherlock-Holmes (2a parte de La captura de Raffles)*, for which six acts of melodrama were required.

Then Lupin had his turn, and again two energetic hacks conspired in the production. Basing their labours on the well-known novel of Maurice Leblanc, Heraclio S. Viteri and Enrique Grimau de Mauro turned out a comedy, *La aguja hueca (Lupin y Holmes)*, and were privileged, Professor Rogers tells us, "to have their effort presented *con gran éxito* at the *Coliseo Imperial,* in Madrid," the date being May 10, 1912.

Returning to the attack, in 1915, Gonzalo Jóver, who had begun the epidemic by his success of 1908, called in a different accomplice—the passion for collaboration on the Iberian peninsula is worthy of a volume—and with Enrique Arroyo achieved a five-act drama called *La tragedia de Baskerville*. Obviously an adaptation of the *Hound,* it was first presented in Bilbao and subsequently in many provincial capitals, "but seems never to have reached Madrid." The authors' delectable instructions with reference to the Hound are reported by Professor Rogers in his invaluable paper: [1]

"El perro ha de ser de atrezzo, grande, negro, de cabeza achatada, en los ojos dos lámparas eléctricas rojas y otra en la boca, simulando la parte de la lengua. El perro irá montado sobre ballestas arqueadas, con las patas extendidas en actitud de galopar. Las dos ballestas se unen por dos travesaños que irán debajo de las patas. Del travesaño delantero se engancha un alambre, del cual se tirará fuertemente, para que el perro corra con el movimiento propio del galope. Para que no se vea el montaje es necesario que los apliques sean más altos que el practicable del camino." [2]

In the following year—1916—Holmes and Raffles were reunited by Miguel Sierra Montoyo in a play that failed to reach the stage—*El robo del millon, o de potencia a potencia (Holmes y Rafles bur-*

---

[1] Paul Patrick Rogers: *Sherlock Holmes on the Spanish Stage.*
[2] *i.e.* The dog, large and black, with red electric lights for eyes and another to indicate the tongue, is to be mounted on arched crossbows, with paws extended as though running. The crossbows are to be joined by two cross timbers, placed under the feet, and to the foremost cross piece a copper wire is to be attached in such fashion that it may be vigorously pulled, to give the animal a galloping movement. Arrangement of the mechanical mounting is to be such that the appliances are not visible from the audience.

lados). It was published, however, at Melilla, and two further dramas of detection—sequels, one ventures to suppose—were promised by the author. Of these, Professor Rogers tells us, there has been no later word.

Closing the list, as far as known, there was presented at the *Teatro Cómico*, in Madrid, in January, 1922, a play by Carlos Grau y Campuzano, in which the author sought to end the series. But it was *Hamlet* without the Prince of Denmark. Sherlock Holmes was absent. In *La última aventura de Raffles* there is the saddening spectacle of the cracksman succumbing to a moral regeneration and giving himself up to justice; but it is one Horacio Katman who effects the capture and not the famous Holmes—a bitter end, one fancies, for the fastidious Raffles.

That there were other fortuitous thrillers in the series, of which available records do not speak, seems fairly certain. No doubt the race goes on; and in imagination one visualizes the astonishing scene—all over Spain, in energetic competition, collaborators working in furious haste upon the latest extravagant *aventuras* of the incredible Ol-mes.

* * *

Upon the screen, the Sherlock Holmes saga has been prodigiously exploited. Most famous, perhaps, of motion-picture Sherlocks, John Barrymore has not been quite the best. That admirable profile, after all, is not precisely Holmesian; and surely the first imperative requisite for the part is an actor who resembles the established portrait. Nor are the lineaments of Mr. Clive Brook exactly Sherlockian, although they are nearer to the mark. When Raymond Massey essayed the splendid part, in 1931, enthusiasts sighed and wondered what the world was coming to.

There have been many Sherlock Holmeses of the stage and screen, but since the first performance of the admirable Gillette there has been only one *face* to stamp the coinage as authentic. It is the face that Conan Doyle applauded, the face which—for the most part—illustrators drew, the face with which the world of Holmes admirers is familiar. The argument is sound. No smart producer would present upon the English-speaking stage a Lincoln who resembled General Grant; no casting director, jealous of tradition, should present upon the screen a Sherlock who fails to resemble rather accurately the public's portrait of that indestructible detective. It is not enough simply to pick an actor who can act, or an actor with a popular reputation, or an actor who himself would like to play the part. Who would *not* like to play it, given opportunity? Even Miss Eva Le Gallienne, one suspects, might be delighted to try a whirl at it.

Mr. Raymond Massey is, of course, an excellent actor. Without having seen the show, one is certain that one should greatly have enjoyed his *Hamlet*, in which—unless report be false—he all but chases Laertes across the footlights, up the aisle, and around the block, in that vigorous, final duel scene of the drama. But whatever their spiritual resemblances, and there is at least an essay in the subject—Hamlet was somewhat of a detective, himself —even the part of Hamlet does not call for as rigid adherence to a "type," standardized by tradition, as does that of Mr. Sherlock Holmes of Baker Street. Almost anybody can play Hamlet, and nearly everybody does; but there are only a few actors on earth, one is convinced, capable of playing Sherlock Holmes. Those few not only *play* the part; they *look* and *are* the part.

It is, of course, entirely a matter of tradition, this ethic of personal appearance; perhaps of sentimental tradition. For oneself, if one had never read the stories of Sherlock Holmes, by Arthur Conan Doyle, had never seen the lean detective of Mr. Gillette, upon the stage, had never witnessed the performances of Eille Norwood and Arthur Wontner, upon the screen, one might have accepted Mr. Massey's characterization—even Mr. Massey's features—with gusto and enthusiasm. Had Mr. Massey played a brand-new picture-story, one might have liked him very well. But Mr. Massey as Sherlock Holmes, in *The Speckled Band*, most famous perhaps of all the Holmes adventures, was a considerable disappointment. And principally for the simple reason suggested: he didn't look like Sherlock

Holmes. As a matter of literal reporting, he looked like almost any nice, young, brown-haired college boy, wrapped in a dormitory dressing gown, smoking a bulldog pipe.

Mr. Brook and Mr. Barrymore were better, immeasurably better. In a physical sense, they did less violence to tradition; and Mr. Brook, in this respect, was better than Mr. Barrymore. Their stories—ingenious medleys of a number of the original adventures—were merely adequate. The "modern" touches did not help the narratives. In the case of Mr. Massey's vehicle, it was the "modern" touches—along with Mr. Massey—that helped to *spoil* the narrative. A Baker Street equipped with dictaphones, steel filing cabinets, and a corps of competent stenographers, is not the Baker Street of Watson. Even the inevitable automobile is an impertinence for those who love the old tradition. Even the telephone, one thinks. When Sherlock Holmes made haste he sent a telegram and followed it in a rocking hansom, urging his driver on with promises of an extra "tenner." His correspondence, we have been authoritatively assured, was seldom answered. For Sherlock Holmes is still essentially a creature of the eighties and the nineties. He is a figure more vividly and typically of his day than Gladstone or the placid Queen herself. The stories "date" as surely as those of Boccaccio and the Arabian chroniclers. And so they should be played and so they should be filmed—with all the careful detail of a costume drama. Only Mr. Gillette, of Thespian Holmeses, has succeeded in avoiding this fatal error of over-modernization.

* * *

First of the Sherlock actors upon the screen was this same Gillette, apparently; he made the film for Essanay, some years before the War; and second in point of time was Eille Norwood, who later played the part upon the London stage. Hero of a long series of popular "shorts," produced—and for the most part shown—in England, Norwood brought to his characterization an excellent reputation as an actor, a phenomenal ability in the use of make-up or disguise, and an ardent personal delight in all the stories. He was an ideal selection for the part. "He has that rare quality," wrote Sir Arthur Conan Doyle, in *Memories and Adventures*, "which can only be described as glamour, which compels you to watch an actor eagerly even when he is doing nothing. He has the brooding eye which excites expectation and he has also a quite unrivalled power of disguise. My only criticism of the films is that they introduce telephones, motor cars and other luxuries of which the Victorian Holmes never dreamed."

Needless to say, when Mr. Norwood made up as Sherlock Holmes, he looked like Sherlock Holmes. His pictures were a trifle slow, but in fidelity to theme and period they frequently surpassed their more elaborate successors. All of the more famous tales were filmed for Norwood, and one at least—the *Hound*—was serialized.

Third in the chronological muster of motion-picture Holmeses was Mr. Barrymore, whose entertaining picture [1] covered a lot of ground. Its most original feature was its revelation of young Sherlock's schooldays—those chapters hinted at by Watson, in *The Musgrave Ritual* and *The 'Gloria Scott.'* Fourth, as the records go, was Mr. Brook, who, as a steward on an ocean liner, painted his quarry's soles with phosphorus, then followed the shining trail through darkened passages about the ship. As a musician, also, in the liner's orchestra, he spied upon his victim, and ultimately took his man to prison. [2]

Most recent of the Holmeses of the screen have been Mr. Arthur Wontner, Mr. Robert Rendel, and the disparaged Mr. Massey. Englishmen all, the alternation and confusion of their releases suggest a merry competition in the studios 'round London. Of Mr. Rendel, who was the burly Sherlock in an uninspired production of the *Hound,* the less said, perhaps, the better. Mr. Charles Chaplin would

[1] Screen title: *Sherlock Holmes.*

[2] Screen title: *The Return of Sherlock Holmes.* The return was merely to the screen, however; there is no connection between the picture and the actual reappearance of the detective as related in the volume of the same title.

have been funnier in the part, but his burlesque would have been intentional. Of Mr. Massey much already has been said. There is left only the admirable Mr. Arthur Wontner.

For Mr. Wontner there can be only words of praise. He has been seen in two pictures, at this writing, in America—*The Sleeping Cardinal* and *The Missing Rembrandt*—but presumably there are others in the making. Since Gillette there has been no such Sherlock on the stage or screen. For two hours, in a darkened theatre, one almost wavered in one's allegiance to Gillette. Surely no better Sherlock Holmes than Arthur Wontner is likely to be seen and heard in pictures, in our time. Sentimentalized, as is imperative, his detective is the veritable fathomer of Baker Street, in person. The keen, worn, kindly face and quiet, prescient smile are out of the very pages of the book. And the direction of Mr. Leslie Hiscott is notably intelligent. In spite of modernization, the tales ring true—so deft, so unobtrusive are the inevitable symbols of immediacy.

In *The Sleeping Cardinal*, the story is that of *The Empty House*, with variations, while *The Missing Rembrandt* adapts the adventure of *Charles Augustus Milverton* to the more complicated necessities of the screen. In both, an admirable Dr. Watson is noted in Mr. Ian Fleming.

It is an old aphorism that familiarity breeds contempt. Like most old aphorisms—which should be reëxamined annually and then thrown out of court—it isn't always true. Familiarity at worst breeds, as a rule, only familiarity; at best, it breeds something approaching adoration. The old familiar Sherlock Holmes, with thin, tall brow and sharply chiseled features, who has become a symbol of all that is best in detection and the literature of detection, is a figure—fictional, if you will—as widely known and loved as any figure, in or out of fiction, in our time. His popularity is grounded in the psychology of the race, whose members are vicariously—as they read or watch or listen—the hunters and the hunted, the shrewd detective and the daring criminal, the great Sherlock himself and the only less tremendous Moriarty; but principally they are that towering incarnation of relentless justice on the track of evil. The tradition is established. The masterpiece is completed. The man lives. To represent him as anything other than himself is to be presumptuous and stupid. There may be occasions when it is well that tradition shall be overthrown; but this, it may be ventured, is not one of them.

The great Sherlock Holmes picture has not as yet been made. It may be that someone is now thinking of it. A word then of advice. Gillette is in retirement, as is Holmes himself—the one in Connecticut, the other on the Sussex Downs. But Mr.

Arthur Wontner is still available. Will not someone send a special, fast steamer for Mr. Arthur
Wontner?

*   *   *

The latest incarnations of Sherlock Holmes and
Dr. Watson have been upon the air. For a number
of seasons they have been immensely popular, in
radio, in the persons of Mr. Richard Gordon and
Mr. Leigh Lovel, whose impersonations have been
admirable.

Sherlock Holmes in Parody and Burlesque

POSSIBLY the most humorous libel ever perpetrated upon the name and fame of Mr. Sherlock Holmes was a drawing that appeared, a decade or so ago, in a leading comic journal. One remembers it with happiness . . . With the utmost consternation depicted upon his familiar features, the great detective is shown upon a pebbled beach, his hand clapped wildly to his brow, what time his tragic eyes consider the stones that lie around him. Millions and millions of them, far as the eye can reach. And underneath the print the artist's casual comment: "Portrait of a celebrated detective regretting his rash decision to leave no stone unturned."

For the most part, Sherlockian travesties—whether in prose, or verse, or line—have been a little cruder than that most whimsical conception. Something, perhaps, of this sort has been a bit more common:

"Ah, my dear Watson! I see that you have put on your winter underwear."

"Marvellous, Holmes! But how did you deduce it?"
"Elementary, my dear fellow. You have forgotten to put on your trousers!"

The lines are not invented for the occasion; they have recently appeared in several newspapers. And they are rather typical of the sort of humour perennially inspired by Holmes-and-Watson dialogue. It is an easy trick. One would engage to write a dozen similar "comics" in an hour.

Between the droll wit of the memorable picture —can it have been by Robinson?—and the humorous vulgarity of the quoted burlesque, much interesting travesty has occurred, some of it signed with names of high distinction. Innumerable parodies of the *Adventures* have appeared in innumerable journals, some very clever, some notably ironic, some merely silly. On the stage the comic aspect has been revived *ad nauseam*, with quilted dressing-gowns and banal songs. In advertising copy, poor Holmes has been unmercifully caricatured, not always by intention; and in daily badinage he is one of the few historic allusions in the repertory of the mob—a symbol as derisively misrepresented as God and Oscar Wilde.

Best known, perhaps, of the more literary parodies is that by Bret Harte, a better parodist than poet, appearing in that author's second series of *Condensed Novels*. *The Stolen Cigar Case* is the title of the story. . . . "I found Hemlock Jones in the old Brook Street lodgings," begins the narrative, "musing before the fire. With the freedom of an old friend I at once threw myself into my usual familiar attitude at his feet, and gently caressed his boot. . . .

" 'It is raining,' he said, without lifting his head.

" 'You have been out, then?' I said quickly.

" 'No. But I see that your umbrella is wet, and that your overcoat has drops of water on it.'

"I sat aghast at his penetration."

The situation is trivial. Holmes's cigar case has been lost—Jones's, one should say; he insists that it has been stolen. There is some amusing dialogue, some absurd deduction, a glimpse of Hemlock Jones in disguise; then a swift accusation, and Watson (or the unnamed narrator) learns that it is *he* who is suspected. The case is found, however, in Jones's drawer, and the great detective, charging that his friend has replaced it there, orders him from his sight forever. At its best, it is bitterly satirical and one of the shrewdest of the many parodies.

* * *

Widely known, also, are the several travesties by John Kendrick Bangs—*The Adventure of Pinkham's Diamond Stud;* the tales told of Holmes's *post mortem* investigations, in *The Pursuit of the Houseboat* and *The Enchanted Typewriter;* and the adventures of Raffles Holmes, burglar and detective, in *R. Holmes & Co.* Years ago, Bangs also did a series of short amusements for the newspapers, which never were collected in a volume, but which for sheer absurd delight were quite the equal of anything he ever published. In them the posthumous memoirs of Sherlock Holmes were hilariously set forth. Imagine Holmes in Hell, with the Devil so overjoyed to see him that he builds a marble palace for the Man from Baker Street and institutes a detective department to supplement the Hadean police force!

Bangs almost made Sherlock and Baker Street his career. And if the general public was dismayed when the detective was reported to have perished, John Kendrick Bangs, one fancies, for all his admiration, received the tidings with a certain equanimity. A sequel was in order, at the moment, to his immortal *Houseboat on the Styx*. In 1897 it appeared, and on its dedication page one read:

"To A. Conan Doyle, Esq.
With the author's sincerest regards and thanks
for the untimely demise of his great detective
which made these things possible."

The houseboat, it will be remembered, with all the women on board, had been stolen by Captain Kidd and his abominable pirates. Great consternation, of course, prevailed in Hades and LeCoq and Hawkshaw could do nothing to relieve it. It was a newcomer in Hades who took charge of the pursuit—"a tall and excessively slender shade, 'like a spirt of steam out of a teapot,' as Dr. Johnson put it." Captain Kidd, he said, had gone to London, whither they must pursue him. He had reached this obvious conclusion by means of a cigar stub. . . . Then he unfolded his extraordinary tale.

"Your name? your name?" cried the associated shades.

The stranger drew forth a bundle of his business cards and flung them as a prestidigitator tosses aces. On each of them was found the neatly printed words:

SHERLOCK HOLMES

DETECTIVE

———

Ferreting Done Here

———

Plots for Sale

In *R. Holmes & Co.*, the amazing hero is a son of Sherlock Holmes and a grandson of A. J. Raffles, "the distinguished—er—ah—cricketer, sir."

One of the very earliest of the parodies was contributed by Robert Barr, under his pseudonym, Luke Sharp, to the *Idler,* a British journal of the nineties. In spots it is immensely funny, at other times a trifle dull. Its superhuman detective, Sherlaw Kombs, is visited by his Watson, who incautiously observes that "the Pegram Mystery has baffled even Gregory of Scotland Yard."

"I can well believe it," retorts Kombs calmly. "Perpetual motion, or squaring the circle, would baffle Gregory. He's an infant, is Gregory."

"This," says Watson, "was one of the things I always liked about Kombs. There was no professional jealousy in him, such as characterizes so many other men."

At about the same time a certain "Zero," writing in the *Bohemian*, narrated the *Adventure of the Table Foot,* ringing another change upon the famous name. . . .

"I called one morning—a crisp cold wintry December day—on my friend Thinlock Bones, for the purpose of keeping him company at breakfast, and, as usual about this time of the morning, I found him running over the agony columns of the different newspapers, quietly smiling at the egotistical private detective advertisements. He looked up and greeted me as I entered.

" 'Ah, Whatsoname, how d'you do? You have not had breakfast yet. And you must be hungry. I suppose that is why you drove, and in a hansom too. Yet you had time to stay and look at your barometer. You look surprised. I can easily see—any fool would see it—that you've not breakfasted, as your teeth and mouth are absolutely clean; not a crumb about. I noticed it as you smiled on your entry. You drove—it's a muddy morning and your boots are quite clean. In a hansom—don't I know what time you rise? How then could you get here so quickly without doing it in a hansom? A 'bus or four-wheeler couldn't do it in the time. Oh! the barometer business. Why, it's as plain as a pikestaff. It's a glorious morning, yet you've brought an umbrella, thinking that it would rain. And why should you think it would rain unless the barometer told you so."

* * *

These were typical of the sort of thing the Sherlock Holmes adventures brought down upon the head of Conan Doyle. But Conan Doyle's own choice among the burlesques—"the best of all the numerous parodies"—was that produced upon the flyleaves of a book by his friend, Sir James M. Barrie. It was for the first time printed in Sir Arthur's autobiography. Doyle and Barrie had collaborated on a comic opera which, in spite of both of them, had fallen flat; and the parody was called *The Adventure of the Two Collaborators.*

"We were in our rooms in Baker Street one evening," wrote Barrie (in the guise of Watson). "I was—I remember—by the centre table writing out 'The Adventure of the Man without a Cork Leg' (which had so puzzled the Royal Society and all the other scientific bodies of Europe), and Holmes was amusing himself with a little revolver practice. It was his custom of a summer evening to fire round my head, just shaving my face, until he had made a photograph of me on the opposite wall, and it is a slight proof of his skill that many of these portraits in pistol shots were considered admirable likenesses.

"I happened to look out of the window, and perceiving two gentlemen advancing rapidly along Baker Street, asked him who they were. He immediately lit his pipe, and, twisting himself on a chair into the figure 8, replied:

" 'They are two collaborators in comic opera, and their play has not been a triumph.'

"I sprang from my chair to the ceiling in amazement. . . ."

It is an amusing enough whimsy but, like family jokes, more significant to its subjects, one imagines, than to its readers. Poor Watson is forever springing to the ceiling, which he tells us is quite dented, and Conan Doyle, the larger of the two intruding brutes, at length gets even with his nemesis, the detective.

Mark Twain, in *A Double-Barrelled Detective Story*, has also had his fun with Sherlock Holmes; but the tale is singularly tiresome and unworthy of its author. Others who have essayed the difficult feat, thinking it easy to caricature Holmes, have been Miss Carolyn Wells, Alan Alexander Milne, Harry B. Smith, and the compiler of these pages. Mr. Milne, reviewing the *Collected Tales* as Watson, is admirable—*Watson Speaks Out* he calls his feuilleton, and we learn at last of the many errors made by Holmes which he, the good Watson, glossed over in his chronicles. Mr. Smith, an ardent Droodist as well as a Sherlockian, gives double measure in a notable contribution to two departments of bookishness—*Sherlock Holmes Solves the Mystery of Edwin Drood* is the title of his paper.

Frederic Dorr Steele, the artist, also has done a parody or two in prose, for the delectation of his fellow members of the Players; and in other lands the number of ingenious travesties has been legion. It was a monumental compliment in caricature that Maurice Leblanc paid Conan Doyle and England—as T. S. Eliot has suggested—in *Arsène Lupin vs. Herlock Sholmes.* "What greater compliment could France pay to England," asks Mr. Eliot, "than the scene in which the great antagonists, Holmes and Lupin, are lying side by side on deck-chairs on the Calais-Dover paquebot, and the London Commissioner of Police walks up and down the deck all unsuspecting?"

In Barcelona there was for years a fiction factory employing a score of hacks, Mr. Arthur Bartlett Maurice tells us, who turned out "Sherlock Ol-mes" adventures by the hundreds. *Sherlock Ol-mes and the Poisoners of Chicago* was one that is remembered; and another was *Sherlock Ol-mes and the Stranglers of Pittsburg.* Tourists in Spain and other Spanish countries—for the penny dreadfuls were imported by Cuba and practically all

South America—used to encounter these surprising pamphlets in their travels, and wonder what on earth had happened to Holmes.

*   *   *

On the stage, as already noted, there have been travesties of Sherlock Holmes innumerable. Most famous of the lines put into circulation by the actors is unquestionably the familiar burlesque gag, "Quick, Watson, the needle!" Precisely where it originated is a mystery; but it first appeared, thinks Frederick Donaghey, about the year 1900, in the wake of Mr. Gillette's immortal dramatization. The success of *Sherlock Holmes* led quickly to numberless skits and sketches having to do with Holmes and Watson, most of which, says Mr. Donaghey, "crudely stressed Conan Doyle's fondness for dwelling en passant on Holmes's hypodermal activities." In a piece called *The Hair of the Hound of the Baskervilles,* written in 1902 for a Philadelphia newspaper, the line was used by Mr. Donaghey himself; but "the gag was old then," he asserts. It was old enough in 1906 for Montgomery and Stone to use it in their Sherlock Holmes fooling in *The Red Mill,* a circumstance which checks with Mr. Stanley Morison's memory of it in a play that was popular in England at the height of the Holmes furore. "The needle introduced was built on the lines of a bicycle pump," he tells us, "only considerably larger." Old inhabitants will hardly fail to remember Fred Stone's colossal pump, or needle, in the *Red Mill* burlesque. For years the line had a popular vogue and was beloved by columnists for purposes of caption writing; then it faded, although now and then it still appears in print. It may be added that Conan Doyle, apprised of its existence by May Lamberton Becker, in the course of an investigation, declared that he had never heard it. Certainly it is not in any of the tales.

Years ago, in vaudeville, at the old *Majestic Theatre,* in Chicago, one heard the late Lee Harrison intone an amusing ballad of no particular melody, the first stanza and chorus of which proceeded somewhat as follows:

> I have just arrived from London—
>   dear old London, don't you know?—
> From my home in Baker Street
>   where I've been looking for the dough.
> I'm that wonderful detective
>   who one night when thinking hard
> Found out how many English feet
>   there were in Scotland Yard—
> I wish Gillette were here;
>   he knows me well:
> Of my exploits you should hear
>   William Tell!

Chorus:

> I can tell the time of day
>   by merely looking at a clock;
> I can tell you if a street car's going
>   up or down the block;

If you'll tell me how old you are
  I'll quickly guess your age;
I can tell an actor every time
  he's riding on a stage!
When a rascally paperhanger
  hung a border on the wall,
I discovered 'twas no boarder—
  just a roomer, that was all!
If your fireplace is defective
Send for me the great detective—
  Mr. Sherlock Holmes is no one else but me!

There were a number of verses equally good or bad, and Harrison—in a dressing-gown and smoking a bulldog pipe—had no difficulty about getting a recall.

Mr. Donaghey's sardonic recollections of the period, informally contributed for this chapter, are worth quoting: "I know there was an immense mass of such stuff about the time," he writes, "and that variety-goers, although few could read, felt that they were getting-on intellectually when, on seeing any one of an hundred actors in a deerstalking cap with a curved pipe between his lips, they were able to say after hardly more than a minute of pondering: 'Ah!—Sherlock Holmes!' I recall one tuneful jingle, in a kids' turn put on by Gus Edwards, wherein the boys and girls of the ensemble came on a dim stage, all wearing the caps and plaid surtouts, and sang 'We're pupils of Mr. Gillette,' the while they fitfully illumined the stage with pocket searchlights. I, helping a friend hoakum-up a libretto which wasn't clicking, wrote a Sherlock Holmes song called 'You Ask Watson: He'll Ask Me'; but it wasn't needed: indeed we tossed it aside before there was time to fit a tune to it."

Weber and Fields also burlesqued the detective, and a hundred others of lesser fame and talent. There are still echoes of the old enthusiasm, from time to time; and no stage detective struts his little hour without a thought or mannerism borrowed from Gillette. Certainly under the head of burlesque must be placed those many productions of Gillette's own play in stock. They may not have been intended to be funny; but they were—all that one ever saw of them.

* * *

In advertising, the manufacturers have, of course, seized upon Holmes for their own peculiar purposes. The detective has been sponsor, one fears, for many curious products, and what is worse incongruous products. When it is merely coffee or tobacco that he endorses there can be no objection; but when it comes to underwear and lozenges—! Occasionally a clever twist is noted, as when George Manley draws that Master Mind in hot pursuit of little dollar marks—like footprints in the snow—until they lead him to the full cash register, symbolic of "additional profits"; but on the whole it must be admitted that the advertisers have been less amusing than the actors.

Among the numerous comic "strips" there have been several efforts also at popularizing Sherlock Holmes burlesque, and one or two, at least, are still in circulation. At times their creators are highly ingenious and amusing; but for the most part the necessities of daily continuity have made them fairly dull. Some admirable single comics, however, have been achieved at the detective's expense; and there are still extant a number of crudely "funny stories." Most popular of these latter—it is quite apocryphal—is the perennial told on Conan Doyle. A cabman is asserted to have taken him to an hotel in Paris, and thus addressed him: "Dr. Doyle, I perceive from your appearance that you have been recently at Constantinople. I have reason to think also that you have been at Buda, and I perceive some indication that you were not far from Milan." And "Wonderful!" cries Conan Doyle, astonished. "Five francs, my man, for the secret of how you did it." "I looked," says the cabby, "at the labels pasted on your trunk."

There are a number of variations of the tale, and one concerns a Philadelphia Jehu, who by his astuteness earned a ticket to the doctor's lecture. Still current, too, is the anecdote of the woman who consulted Holmes. "I am greatly puzzled, sir," she said. "In one week I have lost a motor horn, a brush, a box of golf balls, a dictionary, and a boot-jack. Can you explain it?" "Nothing simpler, madam," replied the great detective. "It is clear that your neighbor keeps a goat."

"There was a third," writes Sir Arthur Conan Doyle, in his autobiography, "about how Sherlock entered heaven, and by virtue of his power of observation at once greeted Adam; but the point is perhaps too anatomical for further discussion."

Surely it must have been a harassed life that Sir Arthur led, beset at every turn by facetious reminders of his infallible puppet. In time he came almost to hate poor Sherlock. But that, in spite of everything here set forth, is an emotion one cannot share.

The Evolution of a Profile

"THAT tall ascetic figure . . . !" cries Christopher Morley, in loving visualization of his favorite detective; and a million voices have supplied the echo.

It seems likely, also, that at least a thousand pencils have endeavored to do justice to the figure. Only a few have been successful. For the most part the drawings have been burlesques; the keen, stern features of the great detective—and his lean and sinewy altitude—lend themselves well to caricature. In the comic journals and in advertising, Sherlock Holmes is a type recognized by infants who have yet to read the adventures between covers. But in the more serious field of illustration the caricature often has been no less flagrant because it was unintentional. Many thousands of words was Watson to write about his hero before a satisfying and sympathetic draughtsman appeared to make the final portrait.

The mental image is, of course, quite clear. . . . "In height," wrote Watson, in his earliest chronicle, "he was rather over six feet, and so excessively lean that he seemed to be considerably taller. His eyes were sharp and piercing, save during those intervals of torpor to which I have alluded; and his thin, hawk-like nose gave his whole expression an air of alertness and decision. His chin, too, had the prominence and squareness which mark the man of determination."

To this early portrait, Sir Arthur Conan Doyle has added: "He had, as I imagined him, a thin, razorlike face, with a great hawks-bill of a nose, and two small eyes set close together on either side of it. Such was my conception. It chanced, however, that poor Sidney Paget who, before his premature death, drew all of the original pictures, had a younger brother . . . Walter, who served him as a model. The handsome Walter took the place of the more powerful but uglier Sherlock; and perhaps from the point of view of my lady readers it was as well."

It must be admitted that the opportunities for caricature were admirable. Yet Holmes was too romantic a figure in the world forever to be a gangling gargoyle, even if Sidney Paget's brother had been less handsome.

Between these statements, early and late, of the detective's sponsors, the facts as to the evolution of the famous profile would appear to be complete. The truth is otherwise. Four illustrators earlier than Paget had tried their hands at that grim, hawk-faced figure, and all had botched the job.

The first was D. H. Friston, a name that is long

forgotten, if indeed it ever was remembered. Called upon to produce the drawings for *A Study in Scarlet*, when it appeared in 1887, amongst others he achieved a frontispiece in which, for the first time in pictorial art, appeared the celebrated features . . . It is a faintly Austrian face, one must confess, beneath the curious flat-topped bowler, yet not without its aquiline attraction; but if one does not greatly mind the nose, surely there was no authority for the sideburns! The scene is that in which Holmes finds the *word,* in blood, upon the wall; the sanguinary "Rache," construed by Scotland Yard as the murdered man's attempt to name his murderer . . . Watson, beside his glittering master, looks on with a fidelity that is as doglike as his astonishing moustachios. As for Lestrade and Gregson, surely they are in disguise? The one a Bow Street runner out of Dickens; the other an amiable country stationmaster?

But it is a jolly bit of melodrama, after all, and the fine dime-novel flavour of it should not be spoiled by criticism. Historically, at any rate, the picture is important—it contains the first of all the many portraits of Mr. Sherlock Holmes.

*　　*　　*

In 1888 there was another. Charles Doyle, Sir Arthur tells us, was a great and original artist, "more terrible than Blake": but illustrating books was not his specialty. Not, certainly, a book of

THE FIRST DEPICTION OF SHERLOCK HOLMES

D. H. Friston's frontispiece to the first edition of *A Study in Scarlet*. Watson is the dog-like figure in the top hat. The others (left to right) are Inspectors Lestrade and Gregson.

which his son was author. Charming it is to own that rara avis, the second edition of *A Study in Scarlet*, with illustrations by the author's father; but pathetic to look upon its drawings. They are the scribblings of a talented child, in spidery lines, upon a wall. Poor Sherlock, instructing his "Baker Street Irregulars"—the only illustration with a profile—is a simple, happy schoolmaster lecturing his truant students, and Watson—"bearded like a pard"—an amiable travesty of Bulwer.

The third attempt upon the features of Mr. Sherlock Holmes was made in 1890—a single illustration by Charles Kerr; it appeared in that year as the frontispiece to the first edition of *The Sign of Four*. An earlier magazine appearance of the tale, though illustrated, contained no portrait of the detective. In Kerr's conception of the tragedy at Pondicherry Lodge, we have a Holmes and Watson beside the seated corpse of Bartholomew Sholto; the scene illumined by an oil lamp in the detective's hand. It is a competent but uninspired interpretation of the episode . . . Just possibly the blot upon our Sherlock's lip is intended to indicate the shade cast by his prodigious nose; it looks, however, like a touch of moustache. For the rest, there is something statue-like and dauntless in the carriage of the famous head; the legs are statesmanlike in their determined stance; and all in all —what with the somewhat epileptic corpse, and Watson—the picture is a trifle comic.

Thereafter came George Hutchinson, an able enough draughtsman, but of the school of *Ally Sloper*. There is a series of portraits from his frolic pen; they illustrate a third edition of the *Study*, produced in 1891—a gallery of caricatures that would have ravished Dickens. For sheer, unromantic disillusionment, one recommends the portraiture of Hutchinson. A too-relentless study of his drawings—they number forty—might even prove disastrously remedial; might lead one to suspect one's judgment and the book! Lovers of Sherlock who have ever wavered in their allegiance, should hesitate before they run this risk.

In time, however, and fifth in point of place, came Sidney Paget. Whether or not his brother was his model, he gave the world its first authentic portrait of the detective. Authentic, one should say, in that it crystallized for the adoring many their own romantic visualization. Today it has been superseded, and those old wash drawings of the nineties seem just a little funny. But after Paget the evolution of the profile was a logical development. The later English artists simply followed Paget . . . Good Sidney Paget! Among the illustrators of his day he was perhaps a second-rater; but he is remembered because he drew so many "Sherlocks." It is a happy enough fate.

His first recorded drawings were made in 1891, to illustrate the serial appearance of the *Adventures;* his last in 1904 to illustrate the *Return.* He illustrated other tales in number, but for thirteen years his principal concern was with the man of Baker Street. It was almost a career. Between the two extremities of time occurred his drawings for the *Memoirs* and the *Hound*. It is to be noted, one thinks, that his later illustrations were much better than his earlier ones, even though—paradoxically —they never seemed to change. . . . Holmes is less handsome in the Paget gallery than Sir Arthur thought him; but he is a familiar and therefore satisfying figure. Less "right," perhaps, than the famous Tenniel illustrations for Lewis Carroll's *Alice,* Paget's Sherlock pictures are a proper part of all illustrated printings of the book, when they occur in England. They are part and parcel of the legend. When death at length removed him from the easel, his successors frankly copied his established portrait; and curious indeed, as rounding out the pattern, is the fact that Walter Paget—the younger brother, who was once his model—was called upon to make the pictures for a later Holmes adventure, after his brother's death.

No single illustrator, since the death of Paget, has so imposed his personality upon the series of adventures, in English magazines or English books. Successors to the flattering assignment—among them Arthur Twidle, Gilbert Holiday, H. M. Brock, Joseph Simpson, Howard Elcock, Alec Ball, and Frank Wiles—have varied little from the traditional portrait, although they have been without exception better artists. And this, one ventures, is exactly as it should be.

* * *

So much for England. In America the story is quite another matter. Here there has been virtually one illustrator only, and one portrait, from the beginning. Still happily engaged at his profession, Frederic Dorr Steele cherishes as his finest professional memory his long association with the lean detective. His portrait is the established American tradition, and is confessedly the portrait of Mr. William Gillette.

Yet Steele was not the first American artist in the field. It was back in the early nineties that Sherlock Holmes began to run his course in *Harper's Weekly,* and in those yellowed journals one finds the earliest American portrait of the detective. Boyish and handsome, with round, smooth cheeks, bow mouth, and curling lashes, the first American Sherlock—in dapper derby and short, well-tailored topcoat—might illustrate a scene from Davis's *Van Bibber,* or almost any story in any magazine. It is a portrait that leaves one startled and protesting; yet in his day the artist—William H. Hyde—was widely popular. His black and whites were excellent in their time. His concept of the long, gnarled Holmes, however, was notably naïve and personal even for an artist of the eighteen-nineties. It is unfortunate that a number of his drawings are still in use, in American editions of the *Memoirs,* when more admirable illustrations are available.

And then came Steele. "Of the thirty-two stories written since 1903, I have had the pleasure of illustrating twenty-nine," the artist tells us, in a paper of invaluable reminiscence.[1] That, too, is almost a career.

What illustrations they have been! No happier association of author and artist can be imagined; one thinks again of Tenniel and his *Alice.* For Mr. Steele was destined for his task as surely as Watson for his Sherlock Holmes. An ardent lover of the long detective, even before he undertook the drawings, his work has been from first to last a labour of affection. . . . Over one's bookcase, holding the first editions, hangs the original of a favorite illustration. The scene is famous. It is Holmes and Watson in the house of Hugo Oberstein, in Caulfield Gardens, solving the problem raised by the theft of the Bruce-Partington plans. The detective's lantern sprays its light along the window-sill. . . . "It was thickly coated with soot from the passing engines, but the black surface was blurred and rubbed in places."

"You can see where they rested the body," says Sherlock Holmes.

[1] F. D. Steele: *Sherlock Holmes.*

No doubt there are better pictures in the Louvre; but at the moment one would not care to trade.

Sixty tales, in all, comprise the saga of Sherlock Holmes; and Steele has illustrated twenty-nine. While yet he lives and loves, and lifts his pencil, will he not do the other thirty-one? To some Sherlockian friend among the publishers, one offers the suggestion—a *Definitive Edition*—with *all* the stories pictured by Mr. Steele.

It is a popular misconception that Gillette, bringing the detective to the stage in *Sherlock Holmes,* brought thereby to life the drawings by Mr. Steele. The truth, however, is the other way round. "The play first saw the calcium in 1899," the artist writes, "but the *Return of Sherlock Holmes,* with my pictures, was not published [*i.e.,* serially] until four years later. Everybody agreed that Mr. Gillette was the ideal Sherlock Holmes, and it was inevitable that I should copy him. So I made my models look like him, and even in two or three instances used photographs of him in my drawings. But while the actor was seen by thousands, the magazines and books were seen by millions; so after a score of years had gone by, few could remember which 'did it first.' I did not, however, see the play until the spring of 1905, some months after my first series of drawings had been completed."

For the most part, these masterly illustrations

appeared in *Collier's Weekly,* in the files of which journal—unhappily—for the most part they still abide.

* * *

But other American artists of note and skill have illustrated the tales of Sherlock Holmes. In isolated adventures or single volumes, as well as in reprints, has appeared the work of Arthur Keller and Charles Raymond Macauley; and one notes the less familiar conceptions of John Alan Maxwell and Patrick Nelson. All have contributed portraits to the gallery, sufficiently traditional and not without their interest; but the illustrations by Steele are the final comment on the text.

In the field of caricature, as earlier suggested, the humorous artists have been busy from the first. It is probable that few indeed of these gentlemen, who have flourished in our time, have failed to seize the glittering opportunity. Ablest of all the masters in this group was Peter Newell; among the most delightful contributions to the legend are his droll portraits of the sombre Holmes, illustrating *The Pursuit of the Houseboat,* by John Kendrick Bangs. But Bangs, who was indefatigable in his pursuit of Sherlock, was served by other caricaturists; among these latter, three names are worthy of attention—Edward Penfield, Alfred Russell, and Sydney Adamson. And rapidly the list becomes a catalogue. It is impossible to name them all.

Presumably, however, some hundreds of competent draughtsmen have added their concepts to the long collection. Among them have been the "reprint" illustrators of two continents; the poster artists of the stage and screen; the ingenious and sensational designers of magazine covers and of dust jackets. The cleverest of daily newspaper cartoonists, and the worst, have added to the gallery. Commercial artists in increasing number still prostitute a great and appealing figure in the exploitation of products dubious and products fine. And one assumes a horde of foreign delineators, in all the fields of art, whose work has never come beneath one's eye.

As yet, however, no painter would appear to have been inspired—a curious oversight. There are paintings of less important public figures in every museum. And there are episodes in the high history of Mr. Sherlock Holmes which, masterfully limned, might make the reputation of some good, unknown fellow, skilled in oils.

Epilogue

SOME time since, the popular Mr. Robert Ripley, writing of the seven most interesting thoroughfares in the world, listed them as follows: Ghat of the Ganges (Benares), Bubbling Well Road (Shanghai), Broadway at Night (New York), the Street of David (Jerusalem), Calle Florida (Buenos Aires), Champs Elysees (Paris), Tala (Fez). Mr. Burton Holmes, given the opportunity, might have added the Street of the Café de la Paix, in Paris, since this is to him the centre of the universe. Sax Rohmer conceivably would have named first of all some opium-denned alley down in Limehouse; it might be called the Street of Dr. Fu-Manchu. But one can not agree with Mr. Ripley, nor with the presumptive selections of Messrs Holmes and Rohmer. It would be quite another Holmes that one would have in mind if asked to name the world's most interesting street. For surely it is Baker Street, in London, the erstwhile home of Sherlock and his Watson?

A drab street—cold and inhospitable; a street of ghosts. A London fog done over into brick and stone. Wherein stalk the spirits of those two departed great ones of the earth. And since there is nothing quite so real as the unreal, perhaps these ghosts walk there with more persuasive tread than any of those other ghosts we call the living. Who is the ragged urchin offering his papers, of an evening, at the Marylebone crossing, when the crowds are scurrying homeward from the Baker Street station of the Tube? May he not be that veritable Wiggins who was the leader of the "Baker Street Irregulars"? And the tall man, sharp of feature, with the eagle glance, attended by the squareset, moustached military surgeon—who is he?

If there be one yet living who doubts the reality of these wraiths, let him write to the Central Post Office, in London, and ascertain how many hundreds of letters have been received, during the last quarter of a century, addressed to Mr. Sherlock Holmes, at 221-B Baker Street—a man who never lived and a house that never existed.

APPENDIX

An Examination Paper on Sherlock Holmes

[Reprinted from *'Life and Letters'* by permission of DESMOND MAC CARTHY.]

1. GIVE the context of the following passages, naming where possible the speaker and the person addressed: (*a*) I haven't had such a day since I had Sir John Morland for trespass because he shot in his own warren; (*b*) Her cuisine is a little limited, but she has as good idea of a breakfast as a Scotchwoman; (*c*) You will ruin no more lives as you have ruined mine. You will wring no more hearts as you have wrung mine. I will free the world of a poisonous thing; (*d*) That clay and chalk mixture which I see upon your toe-caps is quite distinctive; (*e*) You're too late. She's my wife. No, she's your widow; (*f*) Pray take a cigarette. I can recommend them, for I have them especially prepared by Ionides of Alexandria. He sends me a thousand at a time; (*g*) As long as I have my trousers I have a hip-pocket, and as long as I have my hip-pocket I have something in it; (*h*) Ah,

naughty, naughty, would you take a nip at the gentleman?; (*i*) The next word is 'pigs' bristles'; (*j*) You had the proper workhouse cough, and those weak legs of yours are worth ten pounds a week; (*k*) The aortic I may rely upon, but I should value your opinion on the mitral; (*l*) Here it is, written with a J pen on royal cream paper by a middle-aged man with a weak constitution; (*m*) It is a dangerous habit to finger loaded firearms in the pocket of one's dressing gown (*n*) It is not my intention to be fulsome, but I confess that I covet your skull; (*o*) Oh, officer! do let me have a peep.

2. What was *Mrs. Watson's* maiden name? Was she a blonde or a brunette? In what part of London did she and *Dr. Watson* reside when first they were married? Is there any evidence of the date of her death?

3. When did *Sherlock Holmes* masquerade as a Norwegian explorer, an Italian priest, a French workman, an accountant, an ancient mariner, a second-hand bookseller, an opium maniac, a rising plumber, a Nonconformist minister?

4. When did the following serve as clues: (*a*) Curried mutton, creosote, tarred string, a bell-rope (*b*) a thumb mark, a gold tooth, beeswing in a wine-glass, a pair of fresh glossy horses, the last words of a dying man (*c*) a man's height (*d*) soiled trouser knees, a dog that did not bark?

5. Who referred to *Holmes* as: (*a*) Holmes, the Scotland Yard Jack-in-office; (*b*) Mr. Busybody

Holmes; (*c*) This plain-clothes copper; (*d*) The second highest expert in Europe; (*e*) An amateur who has shown some talent in the detective line; (*f*) You cunning, cunning fiend; (*g*) A walking calendar of crime; (*h*) Mr. Theorist; (*i*) A dear kind old clergyman?

6. In what cases does *Mycroft Holmes* appear? What evidence is given (*a*) of his appearance, (*b*) of his habits, (*c*) of his occupation?

7. Solve the following problems: (*a*) Whose was it?; (*b*) Who knocked out whose left canine tooth, in the waiting-room at Charing Cross?; (*c*) Who was the British Government?; (*d*) What took longer being out of the ordinary?; (*e*) Who held a luxurious club in the lower vault of a furniture warehouse?; (*f*) Whose task was it to copy out the *Encyclopædia Britannica?;* (*g*) Who was the most dangerous man in London?; (*h*) Who was the second most dangerous man in London?; (*i*) Who was the fourth smartest man in London?; (*j*) Who was the worst man in London?

8. What light is thrown on *Holmes's* habits as regards: (*a*) Revolver practice; (*b*) Smoking before breakfast; (*c*) Snuff-taking? What evidence is there that he ever: (*d*) Made a bet; (*e*) quoted Flaubert; (*f*) suffered from a breakdown owing to overwork; (*g*) asked *Dr. Watson* to check him if he ever seemed over-confident in his powers; (*h*) acted as best man at a wedding; (*i*) was engaged to be married?

9. When did *Dr. Watson:* (*a*) Recommend strychnine in large doses as a sedative; (*b*) Accuse *Holmes* of charlatanism; (*c*) Characterize *Holmes's* work as ineffable twaddle; (*d*) Burgle a house; (*e*) Pose as a clerk; (*f*) Raise a false alarm of fire; (*g*) Faint?

10. How were *Holmes's* services recompensed by: (*a*) The King of Bohemia; (*b*) The reigning family of Holland; (*c*) Queen Victoria; (*d*) The French President; (*e*) The Duke of Holdernesse?

11. When did *Holmes* use the following to help him solve a mystery: (*a*) cigarette ash; (*b*) a sponge; (*c*) red paint; (*d*) a message in the *Daily Telegraph* Agony column; (*e*) aniseed; (*f*) a bundle of straw?

12. What were *Holmes's* views on: (*a*) The extent to which his own gifts were hereditary; (*b*) German as compared with French and Italian music; (*c*) The merits of a rural, as compared with an urban existence from a criminal's point of view; (*d*) Dupin and LeCoq; (*e*) The genuineness of amber mouthpieces of pipes; (*f*) Flowers; (*g*) *The Martyrdom of Man;* (*h*) The advantages or disadvantages of a stuffy atmosphere; (*i*) Jean Paul Richter; (*j*) Amateur sport; (*k*) Board schools?

13. Who, or what, were: (*a*) Miss Honoria Westphail; (*b*) Tadpole Phelps; (*c*) V.V.341; (*d*) Stamford; (*e*) Darbishire; (*f*) The Fighting Cock; (*g*) Westaway's; (*h*) Pompey; (*i*) Aurora; (*j*) The Wessex Cup; (*k*) Kratides; (*l*) Dawson and Neligan; (*m*) Mr. Cornelius; (*n*) 'The' Woman?

A Final Examination Paper on the Life and Work of Sherlock Holmes

BY E. V. KNOX

[Reprinted from 'Punch' by permission.]

(1) "My professional charges are upon a fixed scale," said *Holmes* coldly; "I do not vary them, save when I remit them altogether." Quote instances to show that this statement was untrue.

(2) What was *Holmes's* number in Baker Street, and where did he have rooms when he first came to London?

(3) For what Rugby football-team had *Dr. Watson* at one time played?

(4) Who, in his opinion, was the finest three-quarter that Richmond ever had? Mention some incidents in this man's domestic career.

(5) To what London clubs did *Colonel Moran* belong?

(6) What were the principal rules of the Diogenes Club? Mention one of its founders. What else did he do?

(7) Contrast the characters of *Stanley Hopkins,*

Gregson and *Lestrade*. Which of them had bull-dog eyes?

(8) What do you know of: The Franco-Midland Hardware Company, Huxtable's *Sidelights on Horace*, the Polyphonic Motets of Lassus, The Royal Mallows Regiment, *Harding Bros.* of Kensington, *Radix pedis, diaboli, Mr. Aloysius Doran,* Yoxley Old Place, the *Sea Unicorn* and the Wessex Plate?

(9) What reason have we for supposing that *Sherlock Holmes* would have disapproved of the Anglo-French Naval Pact? What was his usual attitude towards international affairs?

(10) Who were *Sherlock Holmes's* bankers?

(11) By what chain of inferences were the following facts deduced:—

(a) From *Dr. Watson's* boots that he had just recovered from a cold?

(b) From *Mr. Henry Baker's* hat that his wife had ceased to love him?

(c) From *Mr. Grant Munro's* pipe that he was muscular, careless in his habits and above the need to practice economy?

(d) What deduction was made from the condition of the bell-rope at the Abbey Grange?

(12) Give the context of the following passages:—

(a) " 'My first movement, Watson,' said he as he bustled into his frock-coat, 'must be in the direction of Blackheath.' "

(*b*) "When you see a man with whiskers of that cut and *The Pink 'Un* protruding out of his pocket you can always draw him by a bet."

(*c*) "The boots which she was wearing were not unlike each other, but they were really odd ones, the one having a slightly decorated toe-cap and the other a plain one. . . . Now when you see that a young lady, otherwise neatly dressed, has come away from home with odd boots, it is no great deduction to say that she came away in a hurry."

(*d*) " 'Saddle a horse, my lad,' said he. 'I shall want you to take a note to Eldridge's farm.' "

(*e*) "Lord Holdhurst was still in his chambers in Downing Street. . . . Standing on the rug between us, with his slight tall figure, his sharp-featured thoughtful face and his curling hair prematurely tinged with grey, he seemed to resemble that not too common type, a nobleman who is in truth noble."

(*f*) "Last year I came up to London for the Jubilee, and I stopped at a boarding-house in Russell Square because Parker, the Vicar of our parish, was staying in it."

(*g*) "There is, as you may have observed, a bicycle-shop next to our inn. Into this I rushed, engaged a bicycle, and was able to start before the carriage was quite out of sight. I rapidly overtook it, and then, keeping at a distance of a hundred yards or so, I followed its lights until we were clear of the town."

(*h*) " 'Here you are, Peterson. Run down to the advertising agency and have this put in the evening papers.'

" 'In which, Sir?'

" 'Oh, *The Globe, Star, Pall Mall, St. James's Gazette, Evening News, Standard, Echo*, and any others that occur to you.' "

(*i*) "One night last week—on Thursday night to be exact—I found that I could not sleep, having foolishly taken a cup of strong *café noir* after my dinner."

(*j*) "I have no doubt that she loved you, but there are women in whom the love of a lover extinguishes all other loves, and I think she must have been one."

(*k*) "You will remember, Watson, how the dreadful business of the Abernetty family was first brought to my notice by the depth which the parsley had sunk into the butter upon a hot day."

(13) Discuss the Baker Street cuisine, giving particulars of any meals you remember provided by *Mrs. Hudson*. Examine in the light of subsequent history the statement "eight shillings for a bed and eightpence for a glass of sherry pointed to one of the most expensive hotels."

"There were a couple of brace of cold woodcock, a pheasant, a *pâté de foie gras* pie, with a group of ancient and cobwebby bottles." Who were invited to this supper? Who accepted, and who refused?

(14) Was *Sherlock Holmes* ever engaged to be married, and to whom?

(15) "It was nearly ten o'clock before Holmes entered, looking pale and worn. He walked up to the sideboard and, tearing a piece from the loaf, he devoured it voraciously, washing it down with a long draught of water.

" 'You are hungry,' I remarked."

Quote any other brilliant deductions made by *Dr. Watson* without the assistance of his friend.

(16) "The example of patient suffering is in itself the most precious of all lessons to an impatient world." (*The Veiled Lodger.*)

"Our highest assurance of the goodness of Providence seems to me to rest in the flowers." (*The Naval Treaty.*)

How far do the above quotations justify us in regarding *Sherlock Holmes*

    (*a*) As a great philosopher?

    (*b*) As an expert in botany?

(17) Who was the maternal great-uncle of *Sherlock Holmes?*

A Selected Bibliography

FIRST and Other Important or Interesting Editions of the Tales of Sherlock Holmes as Written by Sir Arthur Conan Doyle.

A Study in Scarlet. Ward, Lock & Co., London. *Beeton's Christmas Annual* for the year 1887. Issued in pictorial paper wrappers, with illustrations by D. H. Friston. This is the first edition.

A Study in Scarlet. Ward, Lock & Co., London, 1888. A small octavo, issued in paper wrappers, with illustrations by the author's father. This is the second edition.

A Study in Scarlet. J. B. Lippincott Co., Philadelphia, 1890. Issued in paper wrappers, without illustrations. This is the first American edition, as far as can be established.

A Study in Scarlet. Ward, Lock & Co., London, 1891. First edition in cloth covers, and third English edition of the book. It contains forty illustrations by George Hutchinson.

A Study in Scarlet. Ward, Lock & Co., London, 1893. Similar in appearance to the above, but with an added Note on Sherlock Holmes by Dr. Joseph Bell, the "original" of the detective. In effect, the fourth English edition.

The Sign of the Four. J. B. Lippincott Company, Philadelphia. The issue of *Lippincott's Magazine* for February, 1890. This journal, published simultaneously in London by Ward, Lock & Co., is the true first edition of this famous story. It contains a special title-page and a frontispiece.

The Sign of Four. Spencer Blackett, London, 1890. This is the first separate book appearance and is generally known as the first edition; it is really the second. The title, it will be noted, has been slightly altered. Issued in cloth covers, with a frontispiece by Charles Kerr. A later issue of this edition, the same year, carries the imprint of Griffith, Farran & Co.

The Sign of Four. J. B. Lippincott Co., Philadelphia, 1890. One has not seen this volume, but one assumes it to exist. If so, it is—unless some unknown piracy preceded it—the first separate American edition. One's own copy, however (carrying the frontispiece, as in the magazine issue), is dated 1894.

The Sign of Four. P. F. Collier, New York, 1891. *Once a Week Library*. Issued in paper wrappers, without illustrations, as of March 15, 1891. Probably the first separate American edition, if Lippincott did not issue an edition in 1890. Numerous undated, early piracies of this title and of *A Study in Scarlet* make identification difficult.

The Adventures of Sherlock Holmes. George Newnes, London, 1892. The first edition, a tall octavo, with numerous illustrations by Sidney Paget. The stories first appeared in the *Strand Magazine* from July 1891 to June 1892.

The Adventures of Sherlock Holmes. Harper & Bros., New York, 1892. The first American edition is an ordinary crown octavo; it contains only sixteen of the original Paget illustrations.

The Memoirs of Sherlock Holmes. George Newnes, London, 1894. The first edition, a tall octavo, with numerous illustrations by Sidney Paget. The stories first appeared in the *Strand Magazine* from December 1892 to December 1893. An edition of this volume was issued by Newnes in 1897 with a new title: *The Last Adventures of Sherlock Holmes.*

Memoirs of Sherlock Holmes. Harper & Bros., New York, 1894. The first American edition, a crown octavo, with two illustrations by Sidney Paget and twenty-two by William H. Hyde. The illustrations by Hyde first appeared in *Harper's Weekly*, in which journal a number of the tales were serialized in America.

The Hound of the Baskervilles. George Newnes, London, 1902. The first edition, with illustrations by Sidney Paget. The story was serialized in the *Strand Magazine* in 1901-2.

The Hound of the Baskervilles. McClure, Phillips & Co., New York, 1902. The first American edition, including eight illustrations by Sidney Paget, only two of which were among those in the London publication.

The Return of Sherlock Holmes. George Newnes, London, 1905. The first edition, with illustrations by Sidney Paget. The stories first appeared in the *Strand Magazine* from October 1903 to December 1904.

The Return of Sherlock Holmes. McClure, Phillips & Co., New York, 1905. The first American edition, with illustrations by Charles Raymond Macauley. These stories appeared first, in America, in *Collier's Weekly*, where they were illustrated by Frederic Dorr Steele.

The Speckled Band. An Adventure of Mr. Sherlock

Holmes. Samuel French, London and New York, 1912. A play in three acts, based on the famous short story from the *Adventures*. The first edition may be identified by its light green wrappers.

The Valley of Fear. Smith, Elder & Co., London, 1915. The first edition, illustrated by Frank Wiles. This novel was serialized in the *Strand Magazine* in 1914-15. The book contains a frontispiece only.

The Valley of Fear. George H. Doran Co., New York, 1915. The first American edition, with illustrations by Arthur I. Keller, reproduced from the American serial publication.

His Last Bow. John Murray, London, 1917. The first edition, unillustrated. The stories first appeared in the *Strand Magazine* over a number of years, one— *The Cardboard Box*—going back as far as 1893. A Colonial edition of this volume was issued by G. Bell & Sons, London, in 1917, at the same time as the regular issue.

His Last Bow. George H. Doran Co., New York, 1917. The first American edition. Serial publication of these tales occurred in several American journals, where they were illustrated by various artists, principally, however, by Frederic Dorr Steele.

Sherlock Holmes. A Drama in Four Acts. By Arthur Conan Doyle and William Gillette. Samuel French, London and New York, 1922. Issued in paper wrappers. First publication of Mr. Gillette's famous play, produced upon the stage in 1899. The printed version differs slightly from the spoken drama as remembered by members of the early audiences; it differs also from Mr. Gillette's reading of the play on his farewell tour in 1929-30, but in no vital particular. First edition still current (1932).

The Case-Book of Sherlock Holmes. John Murray,

London, 1927. The first edition. The stories first appeared in the *Strand Magazine,* for the most part, between 1921 and 1927, where they were variously illustrated. There are no illustrations in the book.

The Case-Book of Sherlock Holmes. George H. Doran Co., New York, 1927. The first American edition. Serial publication of most of the stories occurred, in America, in several magazines, including *Collier's,* the *American, Hearst's International,* and *Liberty.* A majority of them were illustrated by Steele.

Sherlock Holmes. . . . The Complete Short Stories. John Murray, London, 1928. The first omnibus *Sherlock Holmes,* bringing together all the shorter tales in one volume. There is a short new preface by Sir Arthur Conan Doyle.

Sherlock Holmes. . . . The Complete Long Stories. John Murray, London, 1929. The first gathering of the four novels into one volume. There is a new preface by the author. Neither of the above volumes is illustrated.

The Complete Sherlock Holmes. Doubleday, Doran & Co., New York, 1930. The first American omnibus, in two tall octavo volumes, with an introduction by Christopher Morley.

In the above list all volumes not specifically described as being in paper wrappers may be assumed to be in cloth. Sizes have been suggested only where it seemed necessary to avoid confusion. All books not otherwise described may be assumed to be crown octavos.

Studies and Reviews of Mr. Sherlock Holmes in Books and Periodicals, including Parodies and Burlesques, and Other Sherlockian Matters of Interest to the Collector.

Adcock, A. St. John. Sir Arthur Conan Doyle. *Bookman* (London), November, 1912. The *Doyle Number* of this journal, superbly illustrated.

Anderson, Sir Robert. Sherlock Holmes, Detective, as seen by Scotland Yard. *T. P.'s Weekly*, 2 October, 1903.

Bangs, John Kendrick. The Pursuit of the Houseboat. Harper & Bros., New York, 1897. Holmes in Hades; a rollicking travesty.

Bangs. The Enchanted Typewriter. Harper & Bros., New York, 1899. Another *post mortem* burlesque in Chapter 9.

Bangs. The Adventure of Pinkham's Diamond Stud. In *The Dreamers: a Club.* Harper & Bros., New York, 1899. A burlesque Holmes adventure.

Bangs. The Posthumous Memoirs of Shylock Homes. A series of syndicated burlesque adventures appearing during 1903 in various American newspapers. These tales have not been collected.

Bangs. R. Holmes & Co. Harper & Bros., New York, 1906. The burlesque adventures of a son of Sherlock Holmes and a grandson of A. J. Raffles.

Bangs. A Pragmatic Enigma, by A. Conan Watson, M.D. In *Potted Fiction*. Doubleday, Page & Co., New York, 1908. Still another typical Bangs burlesque.

(Barr, Robert). The Adventures of Sherlaw Kombs, by Luke Sharp. *The Idler*, May, 1892. An early travesty.

Barrie, Sir James M. The Adventure of the Two Collaborators. In *Memories and Adventures*, by Arthur Conan Doyle (*q.v.*). A burlesque Holmes adventure.

Baxter, Frank Condie. Introduction to the Lambskin Library edition of *The Hound of the Baskervilles*. Doubleday, Page & Co., Garden City, 1926. A pleasant reminiscence of Mr. Sherlock Holmes as set forth by "Cartwright," the lad who was of use to the detective in the *Hound*.

Bell, H. W. Sherlock Holmes and Dr. Watson: The Chronology of Their Adventures. Constable, London, 1932. A fine volume of fantastic scholarship.

Bell, Dr. Joseph. "Mr. Sherlock Holmes." An introduction to the fourth edition (1893) of *A Study in Scarlet* (*q.v.*). Previously published in the *Bookman* (London).

Benét, Stephen Vincent. My Favorite Fiction Character: Dr. Watson. *Bookman* (New York), February, 1926.

Blakeney, Thomas S. Sherlock Holmes: Fact or Fiction? John Murray, London, 1932. The biography of Sherlock Holmes by a leading Holmes specialist.

Bolitho, William. The Last Bow. *New York World*, 3 December, 1929. Issued as a broadside for publicity purposes in connection with the Gillette tour of 1929-30. Reprinted in *Camera Obscura*, Simon & Schuster, New York, 1930; Heinemann, London, 1931.

Broun, Heywood. Sherlock Holmes and the Pygmies. *Woman's Home Companion,* November, 1930.

Chandler, Frank Wadleigh. The Literature of Roguery. Houghton Mifflin & Co., Boston and New York, 1907. Two volumes. Contains an important chapter on the *Literature of Crime-Detection.*

Codman, Charles R. The Unrecorded Adventures of Sherlock Holmes in Their Relation to the Mental Processes of Dr. John H. Watson, late of the Army Medical Dept. Privately printed, Boston, 1932. A clever monograph containing an amusingly whimsical bibliography.

Coltart, J. S. The Watsons. *Fortnightly Review,* May, 1931.

Cooper, J. A. Dr. Watson's Wedding Present. *Bookman* (New York), February, 1903.

Dougherty, George S. Recovering the Missing Million-Dollar Art Masterpiece. *True Detective Mysteries,* June, 1931. An account of Adam Worth, the original of Moriarty.

Doyle, Sir Arthur Conan. The Case of Mr. George Edalji. Blake & Co., Putney, 1907. A reprint of articles in the *London Daily Telegraph,* illustrating Doyle's own detective ability.

Doyle. The Case of Oscar Slater. Hodder & Stoughton, London, 1912. George H. Doran Co., New York, 1912. Another remarkable pamphlet illustrating Conan Doyle's ability as a detective.

Doyle. Some Personalia About Mr. Sherlock Holmes. *Strand,* December, 1917. Rewritten in part and reprinted in *Memories and Adventures* (*q.v.*). A fascinating first-hand account.

Doyle. The Truth About Sherlock Holmes. *Collier's,* 29 December, 1923. Rewritten in part and included in *Memories and Adventures* (*q.v.*).

Doyle. Memories and Adventures. Hodder & Stoughton, London, 1924. Little Brown & Co., Boston, 1924. The autobiography of Sherlock Holmes's creator; an invaluable and fascinating volume.

Doyle. It is asserted that Sir Arthur Conan Doyle discussed his own detective fiction in the one-thousandth number of *London Tit-Bits.* One has not seen this article.

Dunbar, Robin. The Detective Business. Charles H. Kerr & Co., Chicago, 1909. A pamphlet containing four iconoclastic papers on detection, including *Sherlock Holmes Up-to-Date* and *Is Sherlock Holmes True to Life?*

Eliot, T. S. The Complete Sherlock Holmes Short Stories and The Leavenworth Case. *Criterion,* 1928. An important review. The exact date is lacking.

Ford, Corey. The Rollo Boys with Sherlock in Mayfair. *Bookman* (New York), January, 1926. A travesty.

(Gillette, William). William Gillette in Sherlock Holmes. R. H. Russell, New York, 1900. Illustrated souvenir of an early Gillette performance.

(Gillette). Letters of Salutation and Felicitation Received by William Gillette on the Occasion of His Farewell to the Stage in "Sherlock Holmes." A small volume issued for publicity purposes in connection with the Gillette tour of 1929-30. It was edited by Clayton Hamilton.

(Gillette). Sherlock Holmes. Farewell Appearances of William Gillette. See under Steele, F. D.

Harte, Francis Bret. The Stolen Cigar Case. In *Condensed Novels,* Chatto & Windus, 1902. Reprinted in *American Detective Stories,* chosen by Carolyn Wells, Oxford University Press, New York, 1927. A burlesque, and possibly the best of many.

Jones, Harold Emery, M.D. The Original of Sherlock Holmes. *Collier's*, 9 January, 1904. Reprinted as an introduction to the three-volume subscription edition (Collier) of *Conan Doyle's Best Books*. The story of Doyle and Dr. Joseph Bell, told by a fellow student.

Knox, E. V. (Evoe). A Final Examination Paper on the Life and Work of Sherlock Holmes. *Punch* (London), 31 October, 1928. Reprinted in the present volume.

Knox, Ronald A. Studies in the Literature of Sherlock Holmes. In *Essays in Satire*, Sheed and Ward, London, 1928. E. P. Dutton & Co., New York, 1928. An important critical study cast in the mould of satire.

Leblanc, Maurice. Arsène Lupin versus Herlock Sholmes. Paris, 1908. Translated into English several times. A good translation is that by A. Teixeira de Mattos under another title: *Arsène Lupin vs. Holmlock Shears*, Grant Richards, London, 1910.

Leblanc, Maurice. À propos de Conan Doyle. *Les Annales Politiques et Littéraires*, 1 August, 1930.

Lichtenstein, Alfred. Der Kriminalroman. Eine literarische und forensisch-medizinische Studie mit Anhang: Sherlock Holmes zum Fall Hau. Ernst Reinhardt, Munich, 1908. This important monograph apparently has not been translated.

Locke, Harold. A Bibliographical Catalogue of the Writings of Sir Arthur Conan Doyle, M.D., LL.D., 1879-1928. D. Webster, Tunbridge Wells, 1928. Incomplete and at times not quite accurate, but a useful bibliography nonetheless, containing much of interest concerning the appearance of the tales.

Ludwig, Dr. A. Sherlock Holmes und seine Ahnen. *Sonntagsbeilage der Vossischen Zeitung*, No. 374, 1906. Apparently untranslated.

(Mac Carthy, Desmond). An Examination Paper on "Sherlock Holmes." *Life and Letters*, December, 1928. A brilliant compilation. Reprinted in the present volume.

MacCarthy. Sherlockismus. *Sunday Times* (London), 30 October, 1932. An important review.

Macgowan, Kenneth. Sherlock Holmes. In *Sleuths* (an anthology of detective stories), Harcourt, Brace & Co., New York, 1931. An ingenious brief biography in the style of *Who's Who*.

Maurice, Arthur Bartlett. Sherlock Holmes and His Creator. *Collier's*, 15 August, 1908. The *Sherlock Holmes Number* of this journal, which contains also the first American appearance of *Wisteria Lodge* under its earlier title, *The Singular Experience of Mr. J. Scott Eccles;* a *Ballade of Baker Street*, by Carolyn Wells, and other Holmes material.

(Maurice). French "Sherlockitis." *Bookman* (New York), September, 1908.

(Maurice). Señor Sherlock Holmes. *Bookman* (New York), April, 1915.

(Maurice). The Truth About Sherlock Holmes. *Collier's*, 1 December, 1923.

(Maurice). Forty Years of Sherlock. *Bookman* (New York), October, 1927.

Messac, Regis. Le "Detective Novel" et l'Influence de la Pensée Scientifique. Champion, Paris, 1929. A work of enormous scholarship, which has not been translated into English. A long chapter is devoted to Sherlock Holmes, who is frequently mentioned throughout the book.

Milne, A. A. Dr. Watson Speaks Out. *Nation & Athenæum*, 17 November, 1928. Reprinted in his volume of essays, *By Way of Introduction*. A review of the omnibus *Sherlock Holmes* as it might have been done by Dr. Watson.

Mitchell, Basil. The Holmeses of Baker Street. A play produced at the Lyric Theatre, London, in February 1933. Unpublished.

Mitchell (with Frederic Arnold Kummer). The Adventure of the Queen Bee. A novelization of the above. Serialized in *The Mystery Magazine,* beginning July, 1933. The play and the novel introduce daughters of Sherlock Holmes and Dr. Watson in a modern setting.

Morley, Christopher. In Memoriam: Sherlock Holmes. *Saturday Review of Literature* (New York), 2 August, 1930. Reprinted as an introduction to the *Complete Sherlock Holmes,* Doubleday, Doran & Co., New York, 1930.

Park, William. The Truth About Oscar Slater. With an introduction by Sir Arthur Conan Doyle. The Psychic Press, London, n.d. Conan Doyle as Sherlock Holmes.

Parsons, Alan. A Word, my dear Watson, in your Defense: a reasoned plea for the famous Foil who played Boswell to Sherlock Holmes's Johnson. *Britannia and Eve,* December, 1932.

Peck, Harry Thurston. A Chat About Sherlock Holmes. *Independent,* 21 November, 1901.

Pearson, Edmund. Ave atque vale, Sherlock! *Outlook* (New York), 20 July, 1927.

Pearson. Sherlock Holmes Among the Illustrators. *Bookman* (New York), August, 1932.

Rendall, Vernon. The London Nights of Belsize. John Lane, London, 1917. Contains a chapter on the methods of Sherlock Holmes.

(Roberts, S. C.). A Note on the Watson Problem. A

privately printed pamphlet (100 copies), University Press, Cambridge (England), 1929. A retort to Father Knox's *Studies in the Literature of Sherlock Holmes* (*q.v.*).

Roberts, S. C. Doctor Watson. Prologomena to the study of a biographical problem, with a bibliography of Sherlock Holmes. Faber & Faber, London, 1931. A gorgeous serio-comic biography of the good Watson.

Roberts. The Watson Problem. *Observer,* 30 October, 1932. An important review.

Rogers, Paul Patrick. Sherlock Holmes on the Spanish Stage. *Modern Language Forum,* June, 1931.

(Saxby, Jessie M. E.). Joseph Bell, M.D., F.R.C.S., J.P., D.L., Etc. An Appreciation by an Old Friend. Oliphant, Anderson & Ferrier, Edinburgh, 1913. An illustrated biography of the "original" of Sherlock Holmes.

Sayers, Dorothy L. Great Short Stories of Detection, Mystery and Horror. Victor Gollancz, London, 1928. This remarkable anthology contains a long and important historical introduction in which Holmes plays his part.

Shanks, Edward. "You Know My Methods, Watson." *John o' London's Weekly,* 17 November, 1928.

Shanks. Conan Doyle. An Appreciation of the Creator of "Sherlock Holmes." *John o' London's Weekly,* 26 July, 1930. This issue, a memorial to the dead author, contains also *Conan Doyle and the Unknown* (unsigned) and a reprint of *The Red-Headed League.*

Sherie, Fenn. Sherlock Holmes on the Film: An Interview with Eille Norwood. *Strand,* ——, 192– (?).

Sherlockholmitos. *Times Literary Supplement* (London). 27 October, 1932. An unsigned review of great interest and scholarship.

Smith, Harry B. Sherlock Holmes Solves the Mystery of Edwin Drood. *Munsey's Magazine,* December, 1924. A jolly idea, but Mr. Smith had been anticipated. In *Longman's Magazine* for September, 1905, appeared an anonymous *Interview between Dr. Watson and Sherlock Holmes on the Drood Mystery.*

Stark, B. How Old is Sherlock Holmes? *Bookman* (New York), July, 1920.

Starrett, Vincent. In Praise of Sherlock Holmes. *Reedy's Mirror* (St. Louis), 22 February, 1918.

Starrett. The Unique Hamlet: a hitherto unchronicled adventure of Mr. Sherlock Holmes. Walter M. Hill, Chicago, 1920. Privately printed (200 copies) by the Torch Press. A satire on book collecting.

Starrett. The Real Sherlock Holmes. *Golden Book,* December, 1930. Reprinted, with additions, in this volume. The magazine contains also a finely illustrated reprint of *The Speckled Band,* the drawings by John Alan Maxwell.

Starrett. Enter Mr. Sherlock Holmes. *Atlantic,* July, 1932. Reprinted in this volume.

Starrett. Mr. Holmes of Baker Street. *Real Detective,* December, 1932. Reprinted in this volume as *No. 221-B Baker Street.*

Starrett. The Private Life of Sherlock Holmes. *Bookman* (New York), December, 1932. Reprinted in this volume.

Starrett. Sherlock Holmes: Notes for a Biography. *Bookman* (New York), February, 1933. Reprinted in this volume, with additions, as *Ave Sherlock Morituri et Cetera.*

Steele, Frederic Dorr. Sherlock Holmes. Farewell Appearances of William Gillette, 1929-1930. New York, 1929. An illustrated souvenir booklet issued in connection with Gillette's tour. Packed with information and admirably illustrated, it is of the highest interest and importance to collectors. A second edition has been revised and contains a note on Doyle's death.

Thomson, H. Douglas. Masters of Mystery. A Study of the Detective Story. W. Collins Sons & Co., London, 1931. A valuable book, with a chapter on Sherlock Holmes.

Twain, Mark. A Double-Barrelled Detective Story. Harper & Bros., New York, 1902. A burlesque Western melodrama introducing Sherlock Holmes.

Wells, Carolyn. The Technique of the Mystery Story. Home Correspondence School, Springfield (Mass.), 1913. New and revised edition, 1929. A fascinating volume of detective lore, with much to say of Sherlock Holmes.

Wells. The Adventure of the Clothes Line. *Century Magazine,* May, 1915. A burlesque detective story introducing Holmes as president of a society of infallible detectives.

Wright, Willard Huntington. The Great Detective Stories. Scribner, New York, 1927. A notable anthology, containing a long and important historical introduction in which Holmes has his place.

Wrong, E. M. Crime and Detection. Oxford University Press, 1926. An excellent anthology of detective stories, with an interesting introduction containing good talk of Sherlock Holmes.

"Zero." The Adventure of the Table Foot. *Bohemian* (London), January, 1894. An early travesty.

[It should be emphasized that the foregoing short bibliography does not attempt to list even a one-hundredth part of the many books, pamphlets, articles, burlesques, editorials, and other writings about Sherlock Holmes. For the most part the task has been a matter of selecting the more interesting and most important of the several hundred items in the author's own collection.]